Oddities of a Strange Mind
By Matthew E. Breer

An adult coloring book, Inspired by illustrations of old!

Over 40 illustrations for hours of stress relieving fun!

This book makes a perfect gift for everyone!

Be sure to check us out on Facebook and our website for other great things!

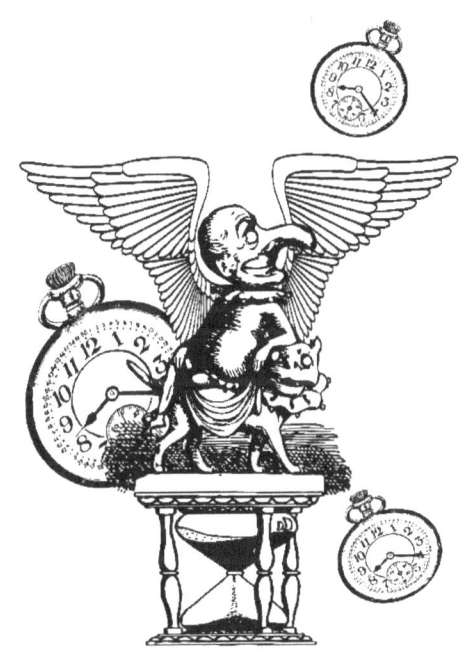

http://breerspublishing.weebly.com/

https://www.facebook.com/BreersPublishing/

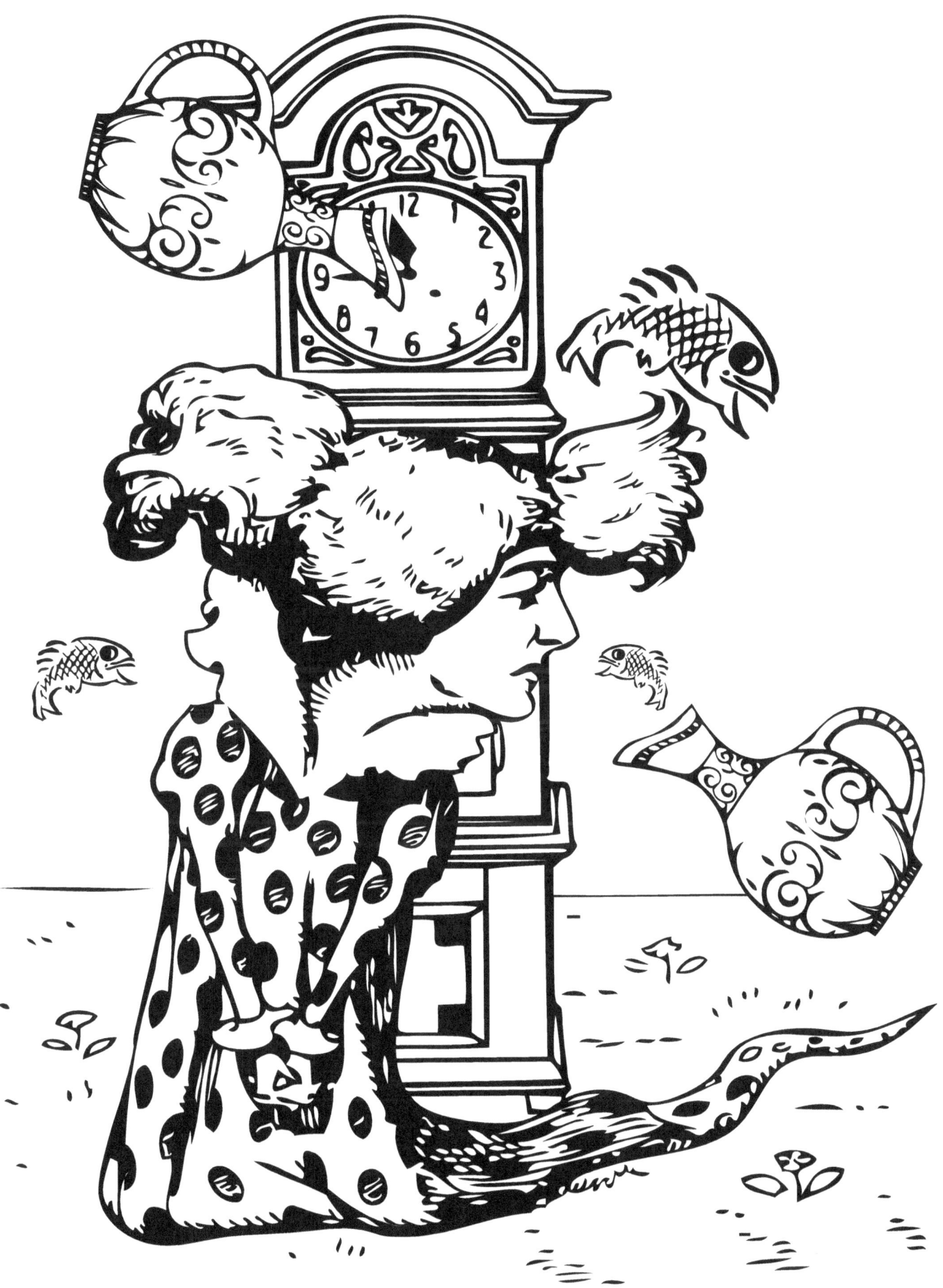

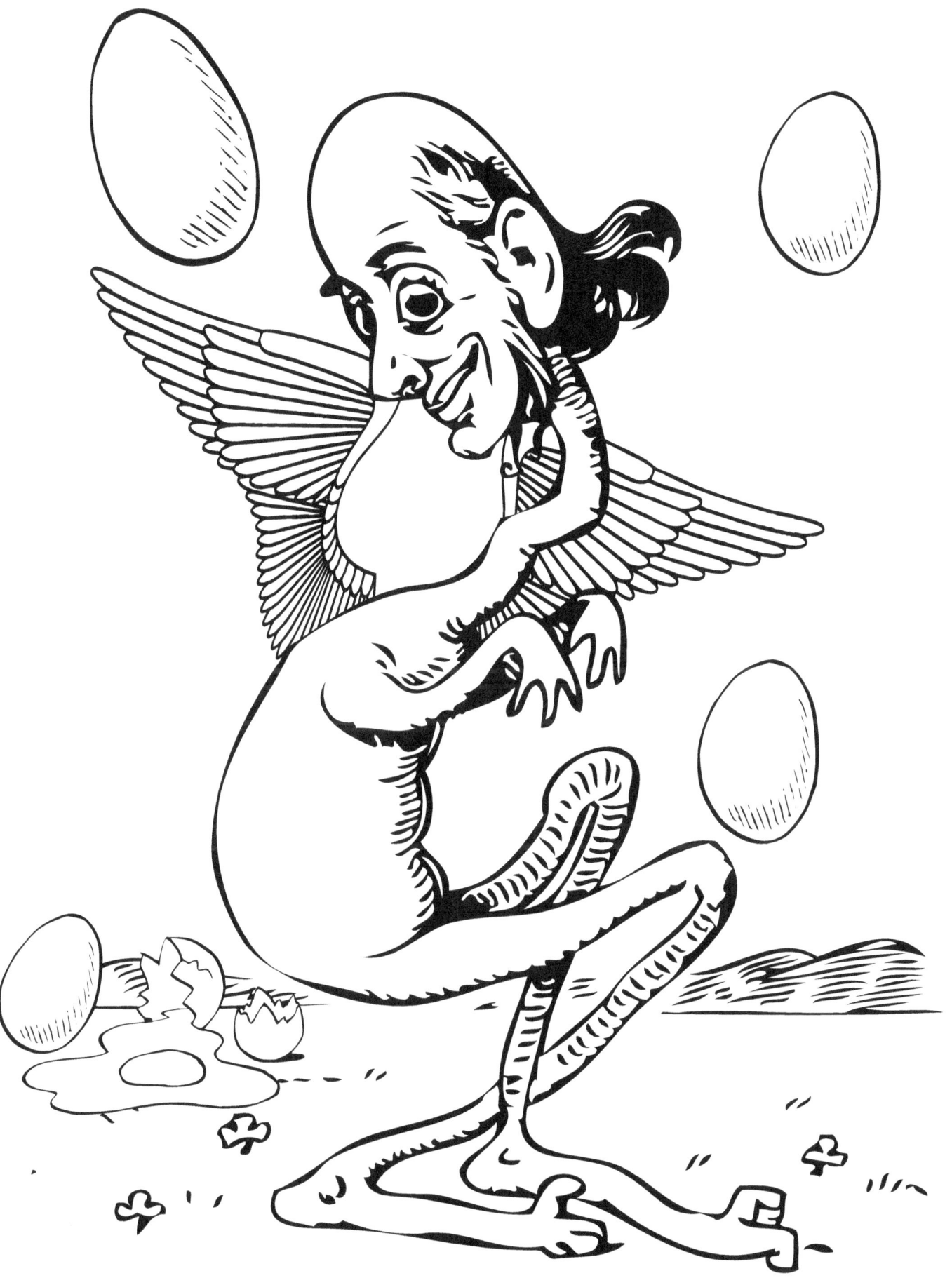

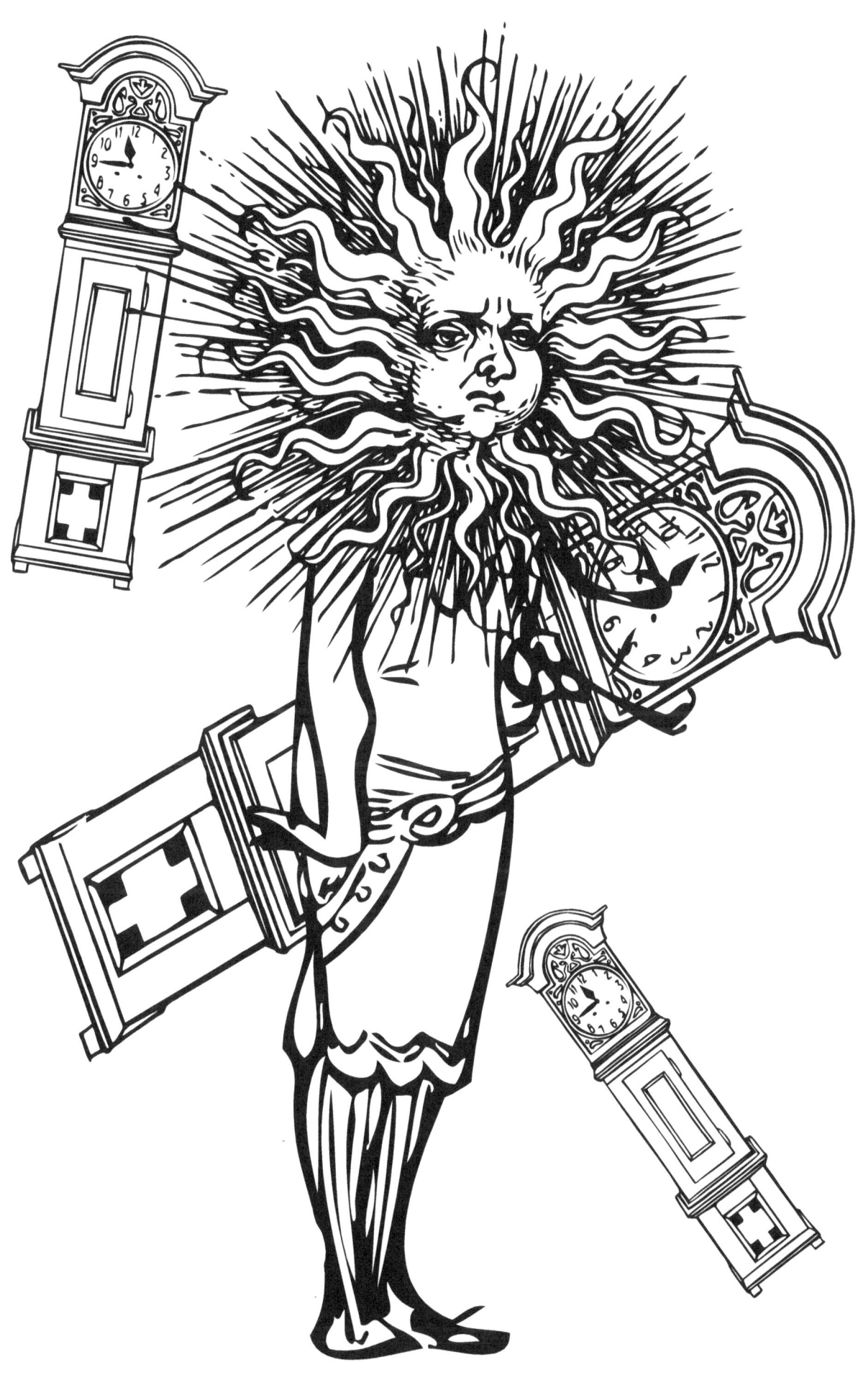

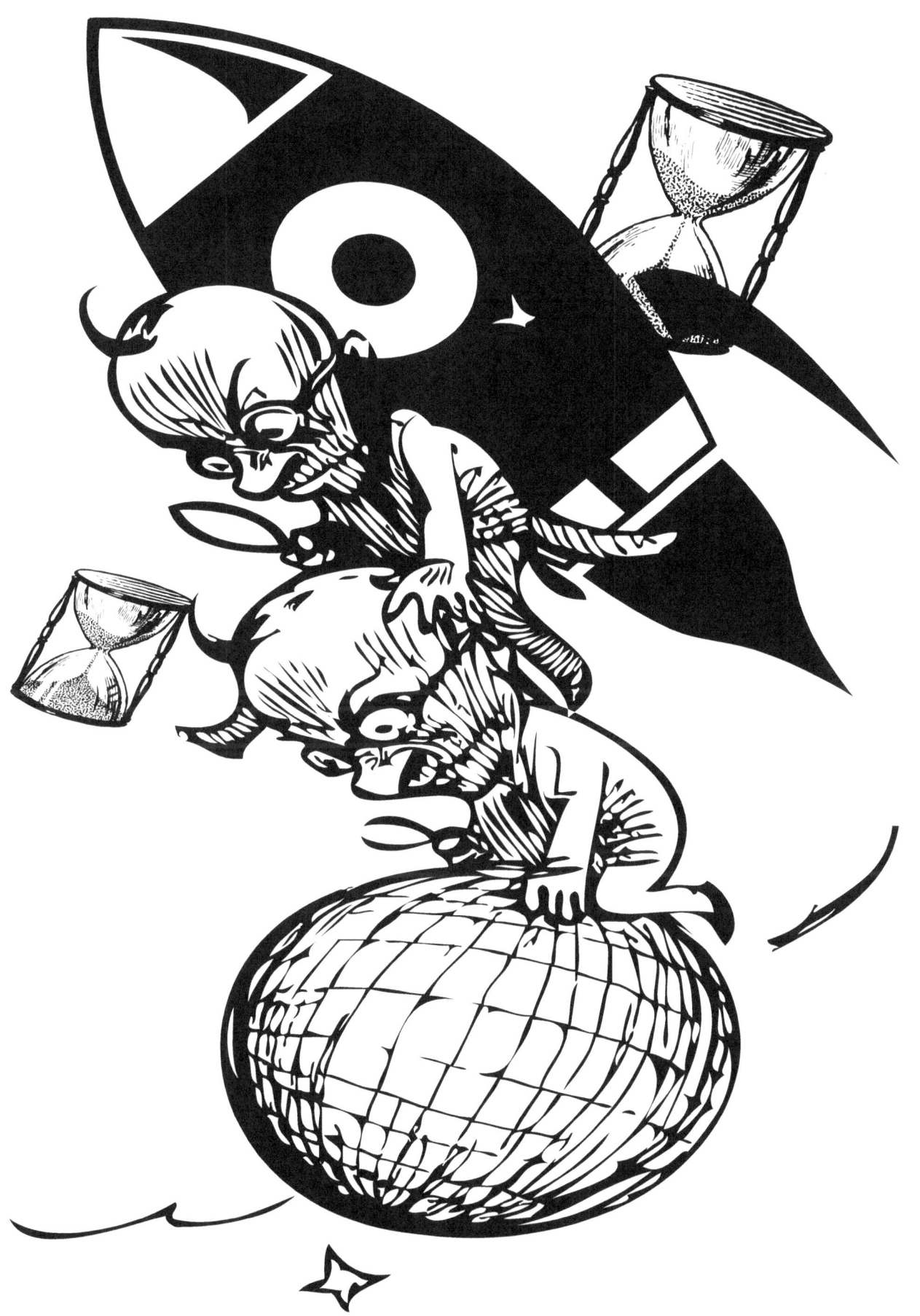

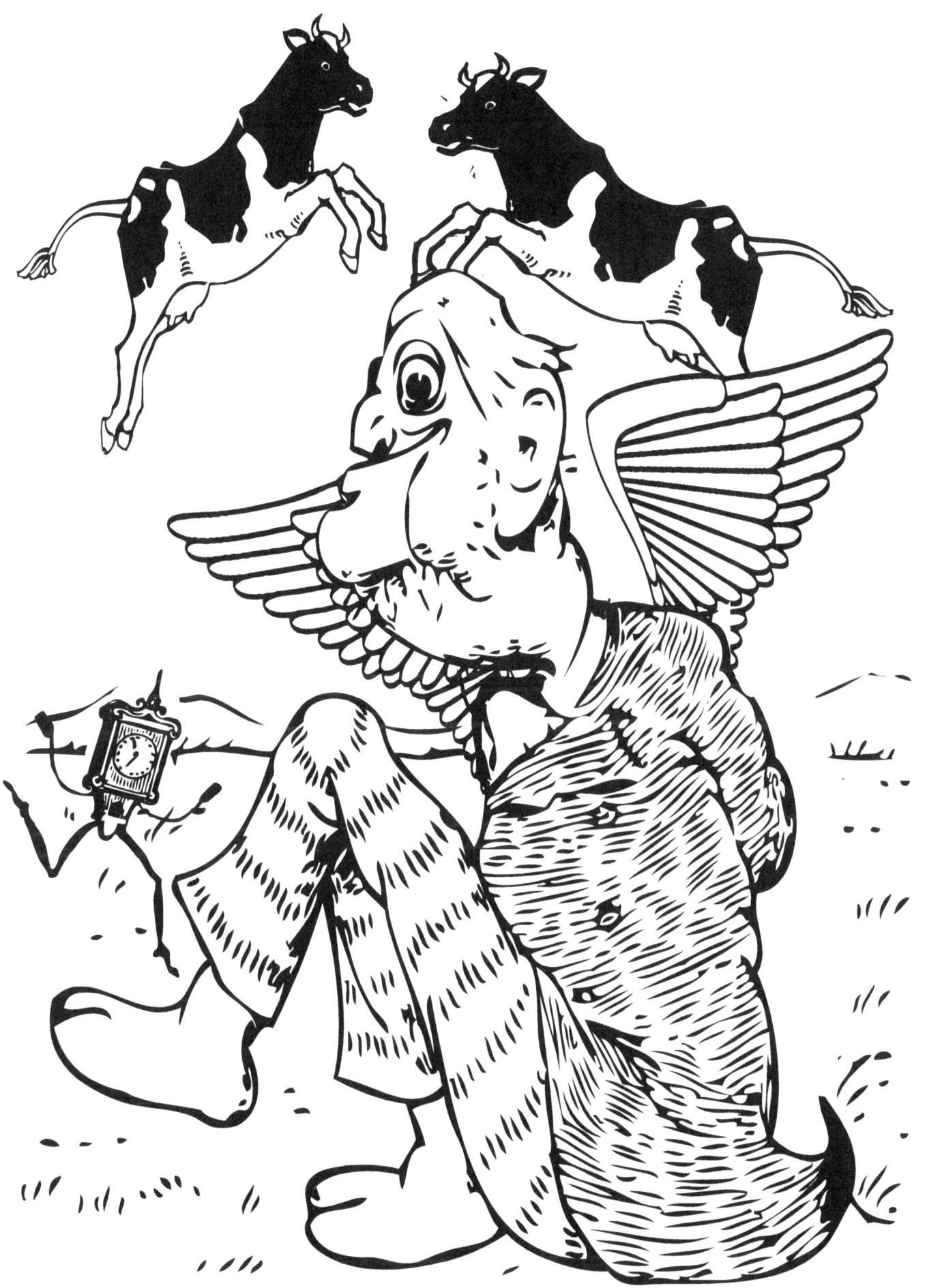

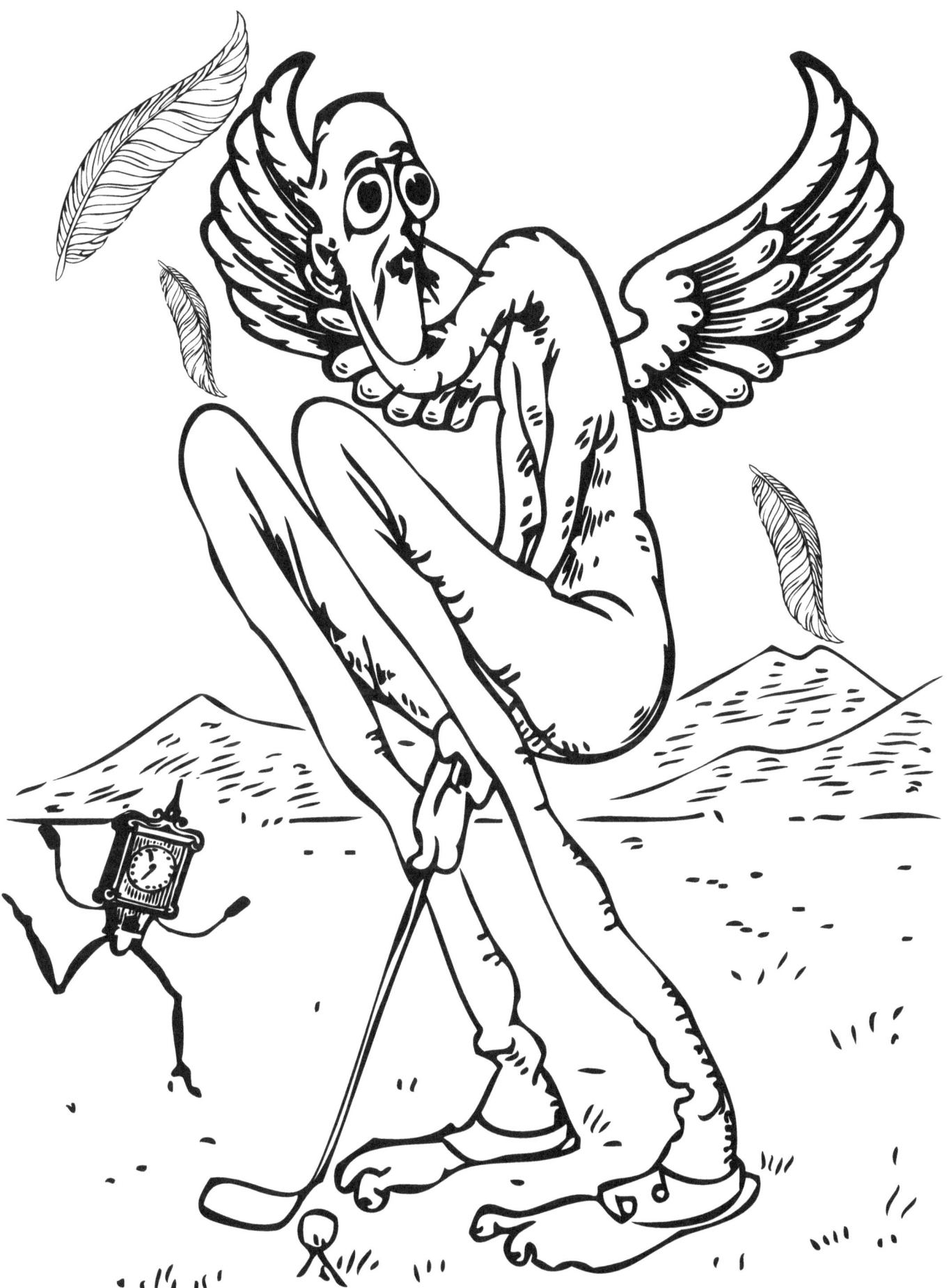

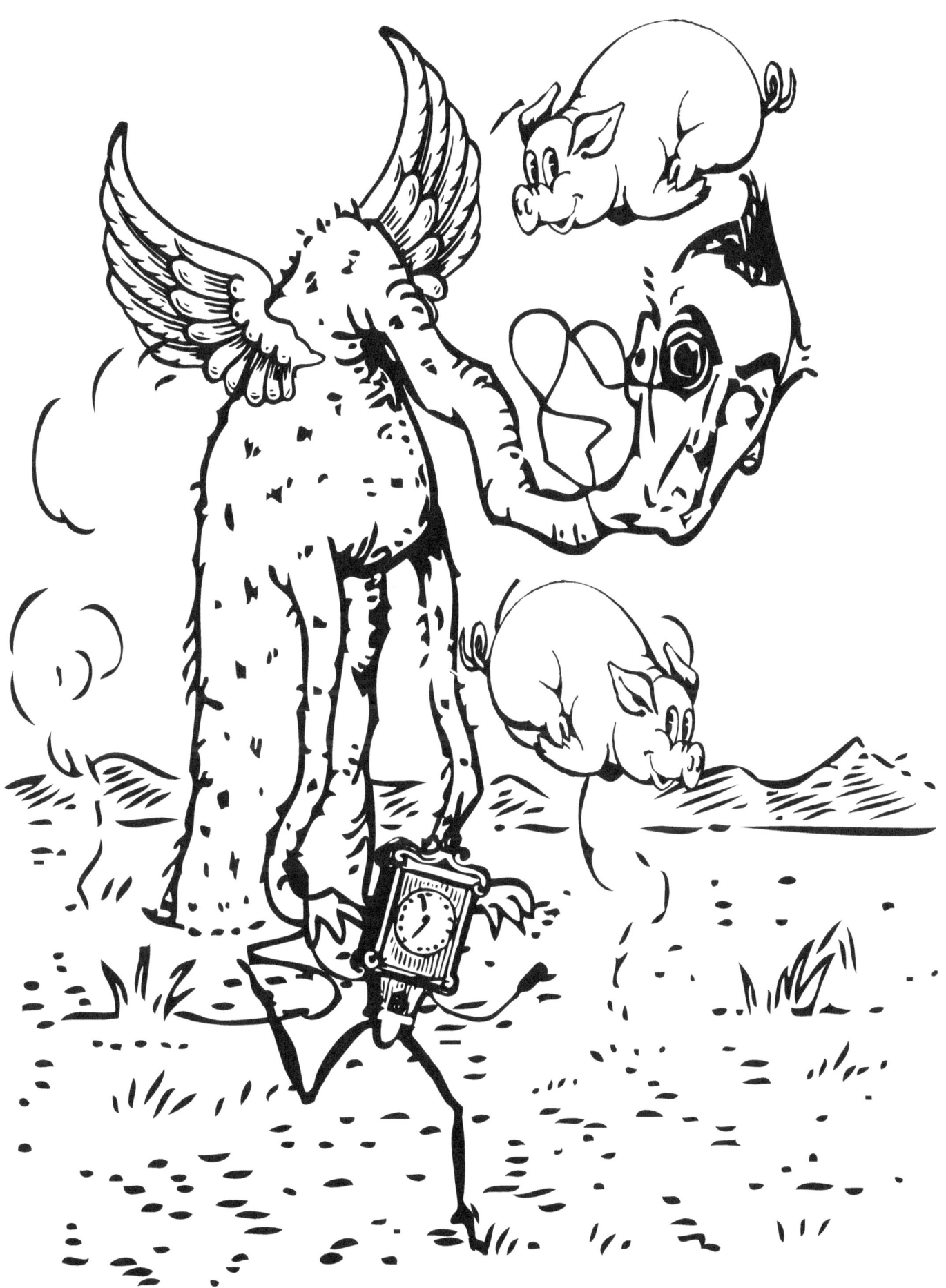

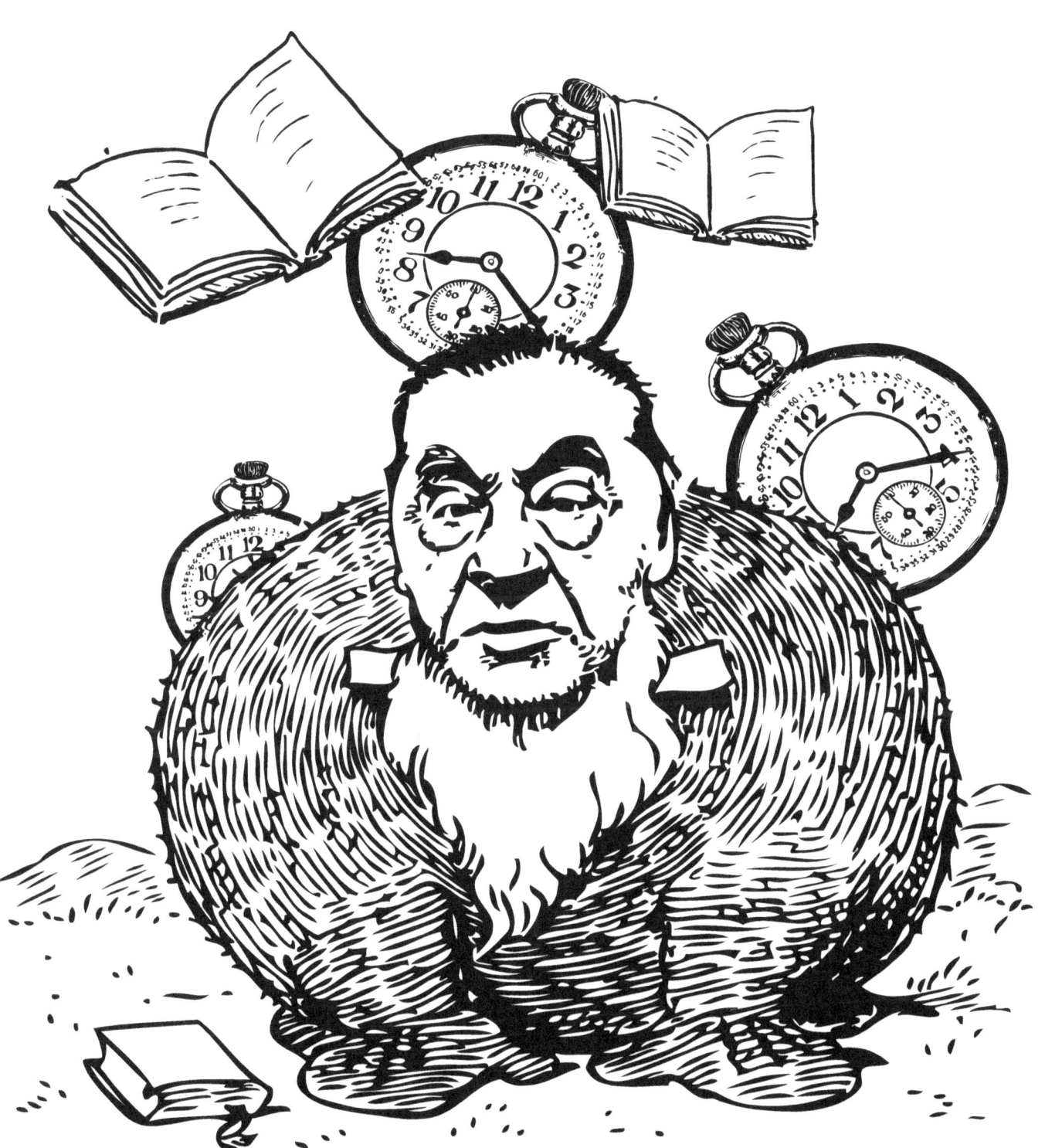

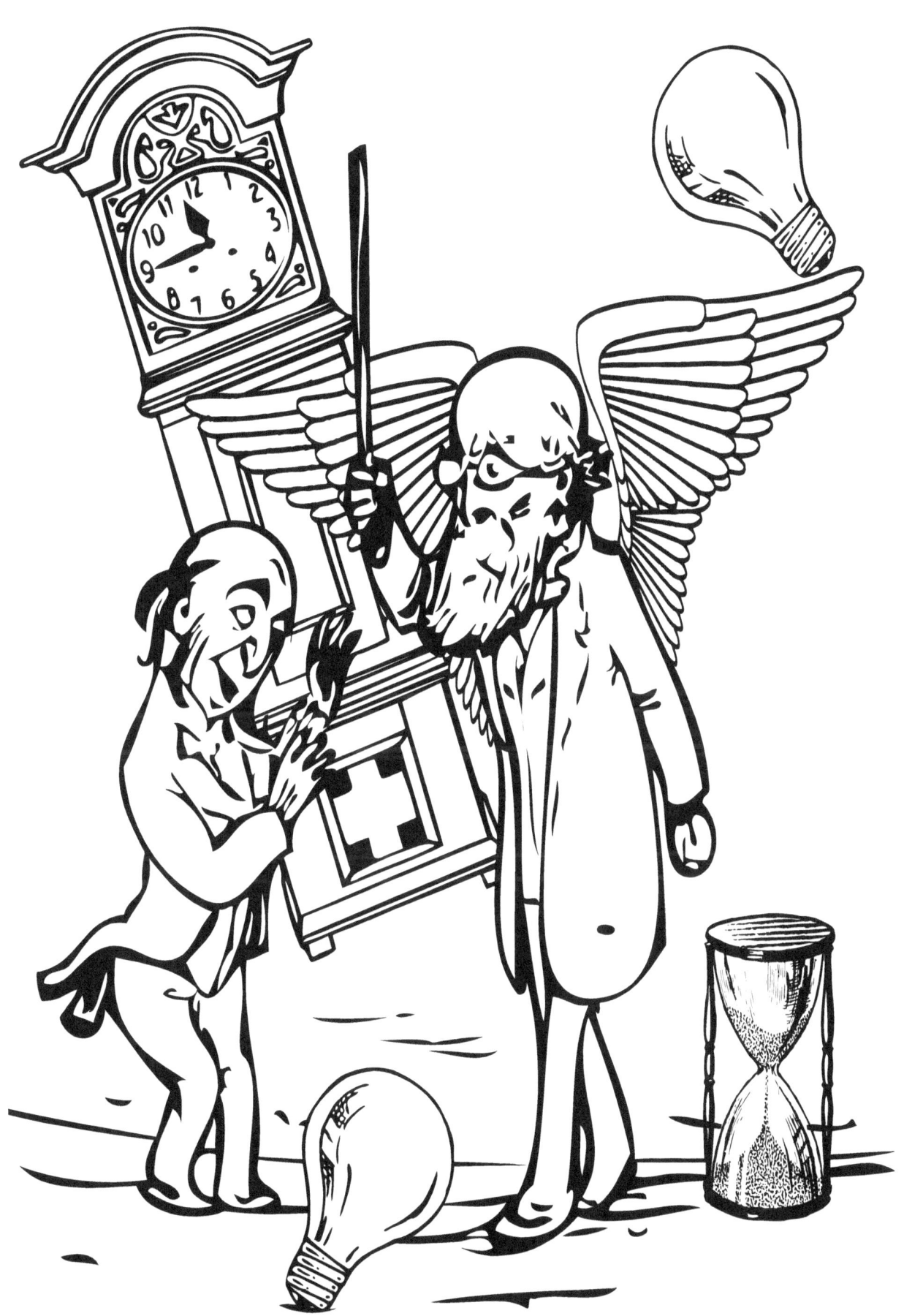

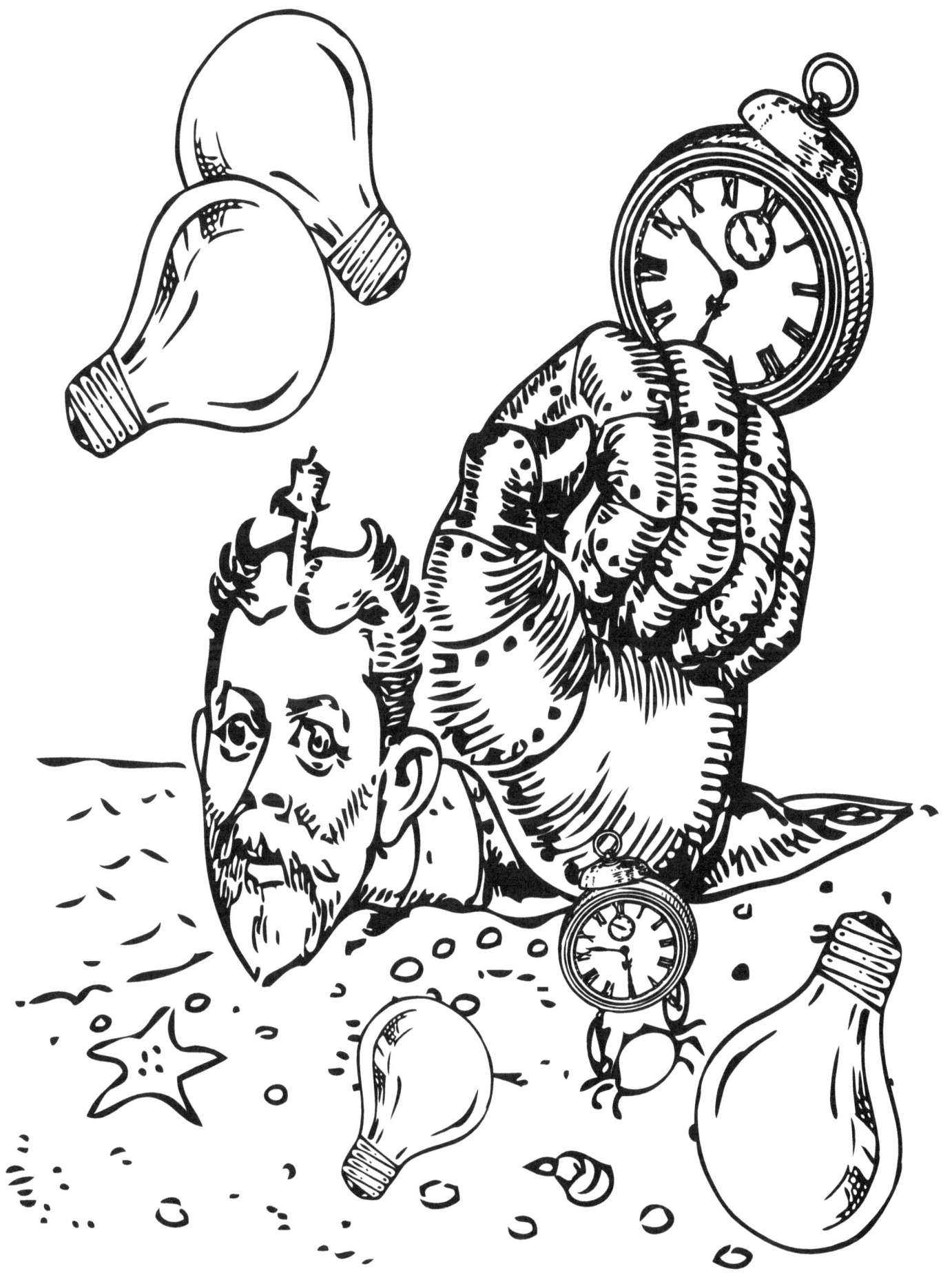

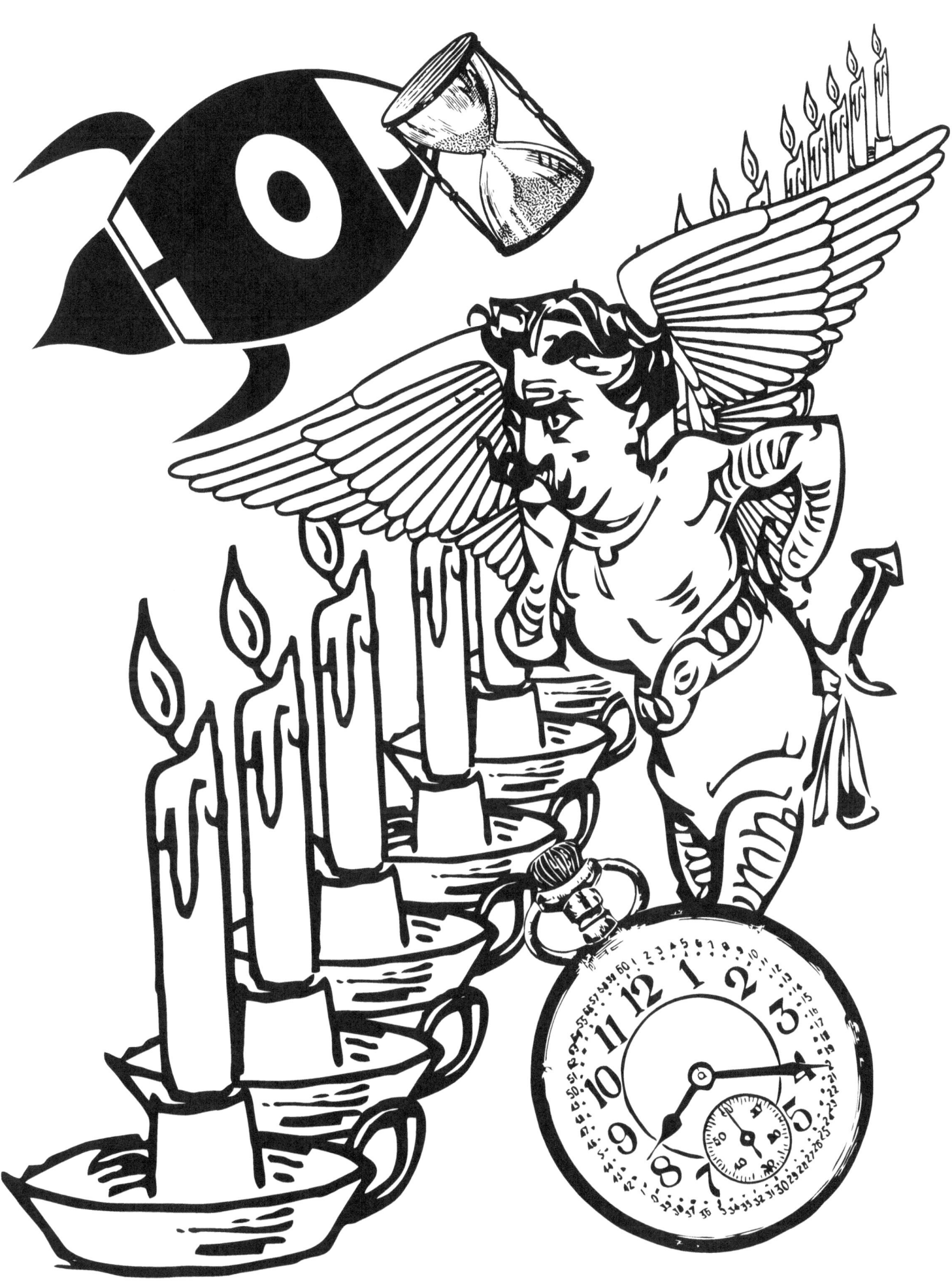

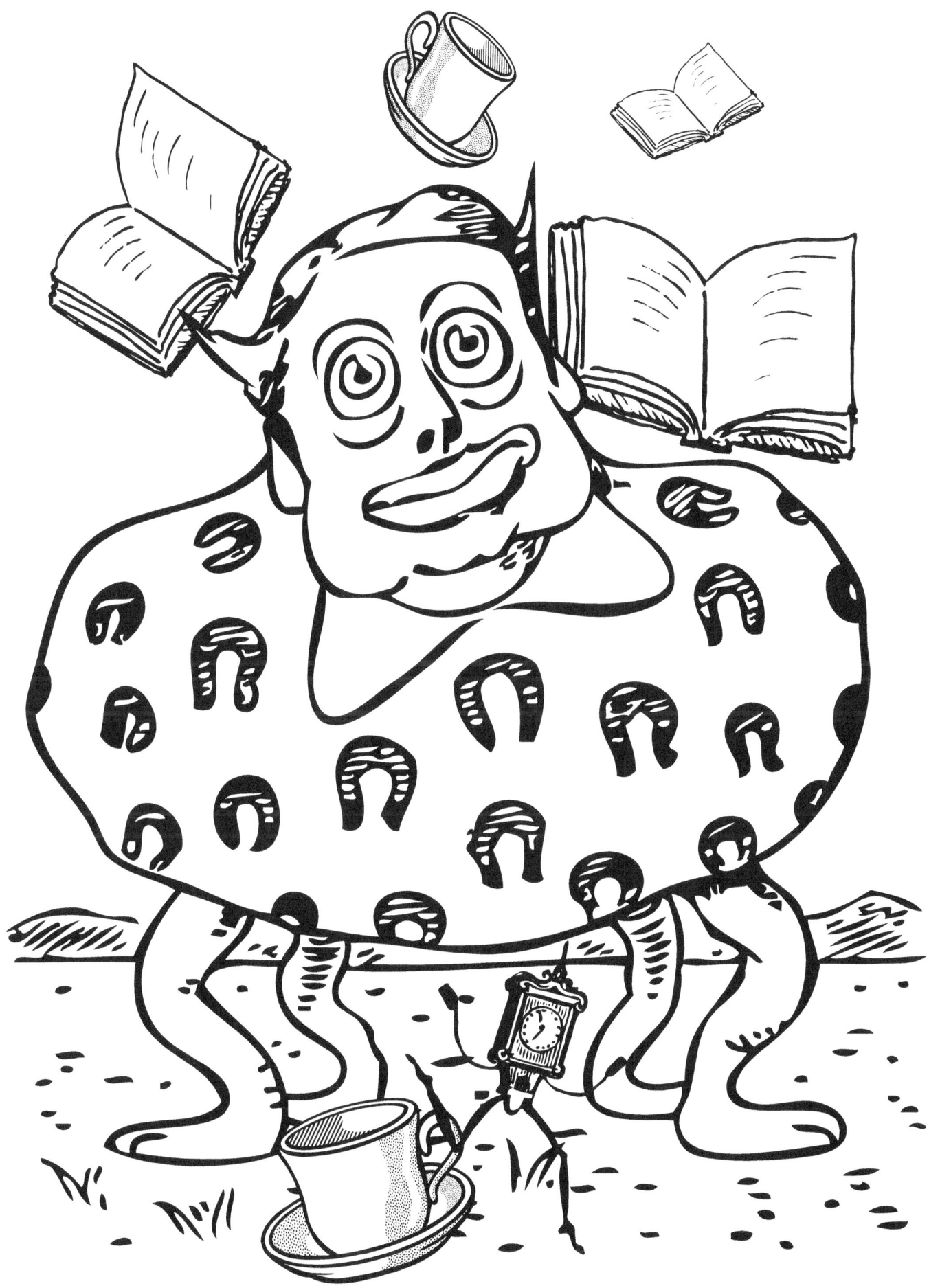

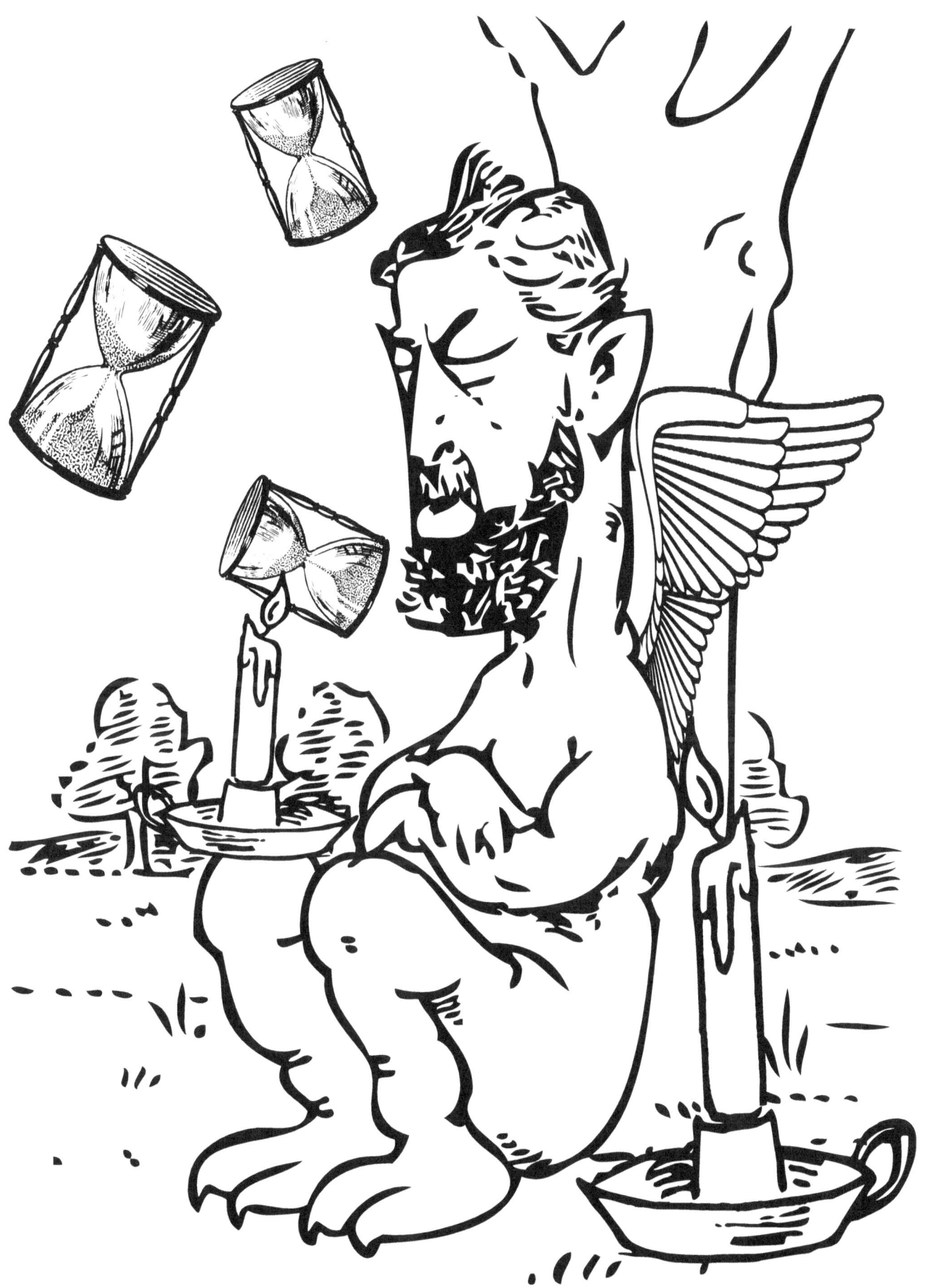

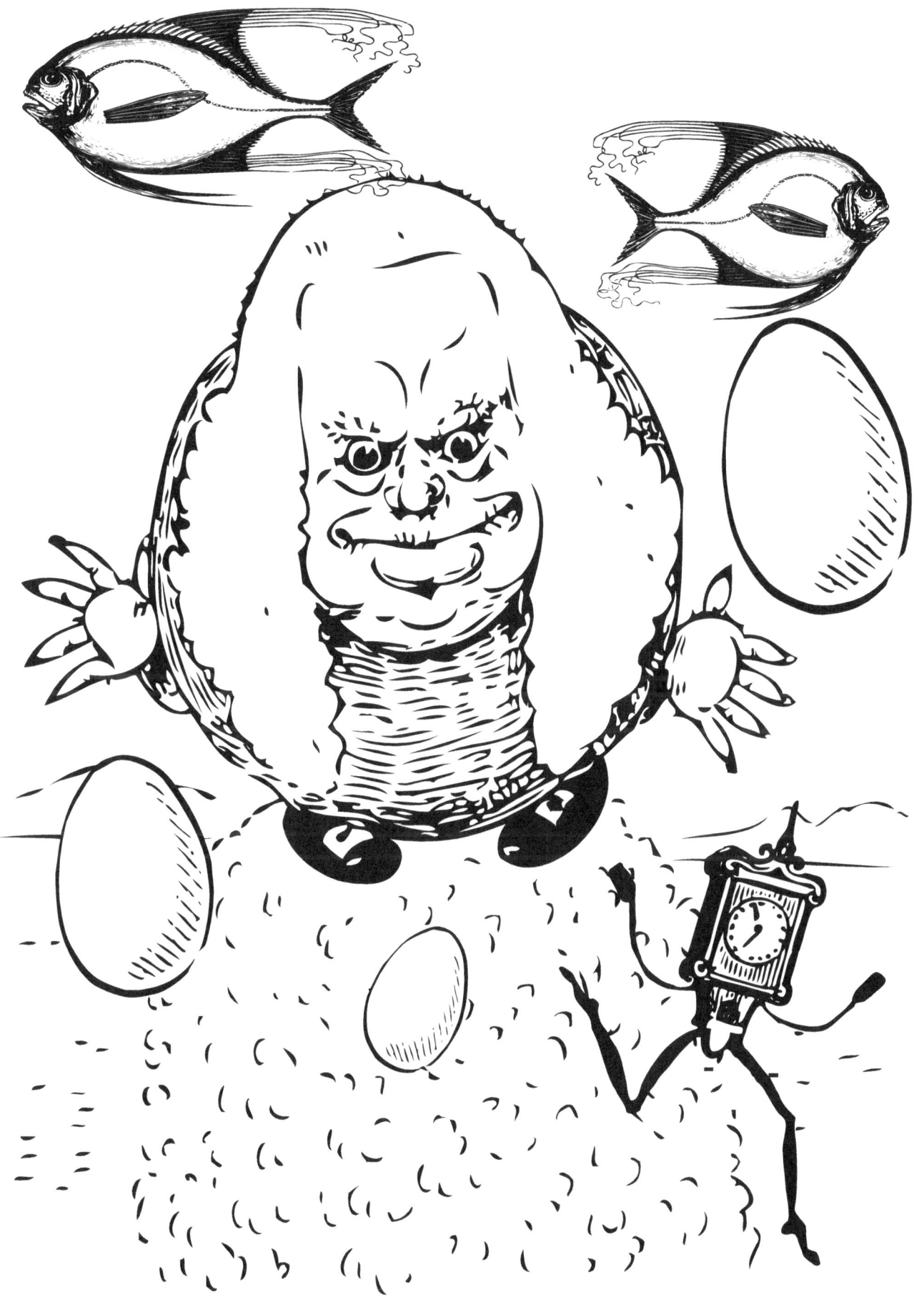

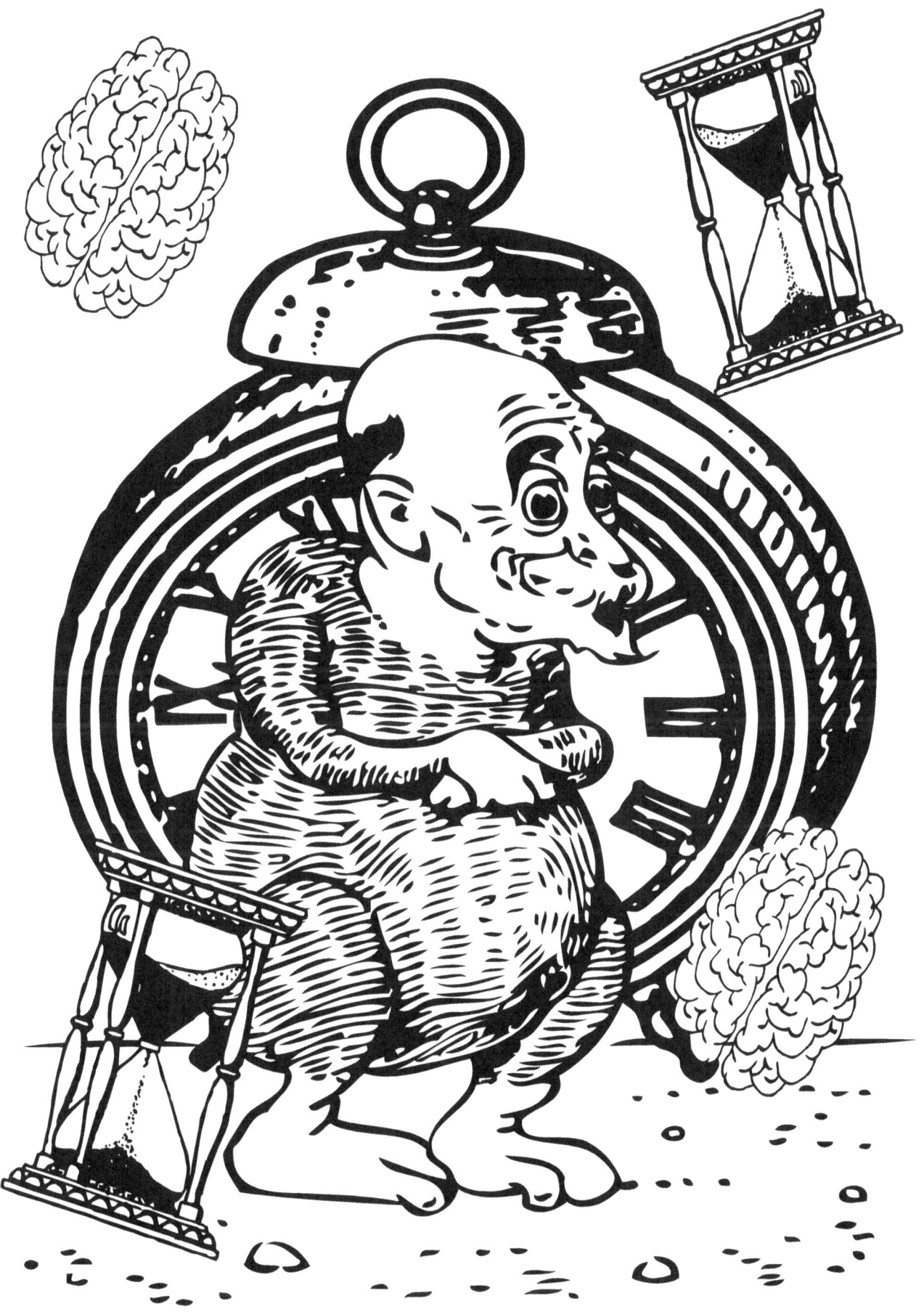

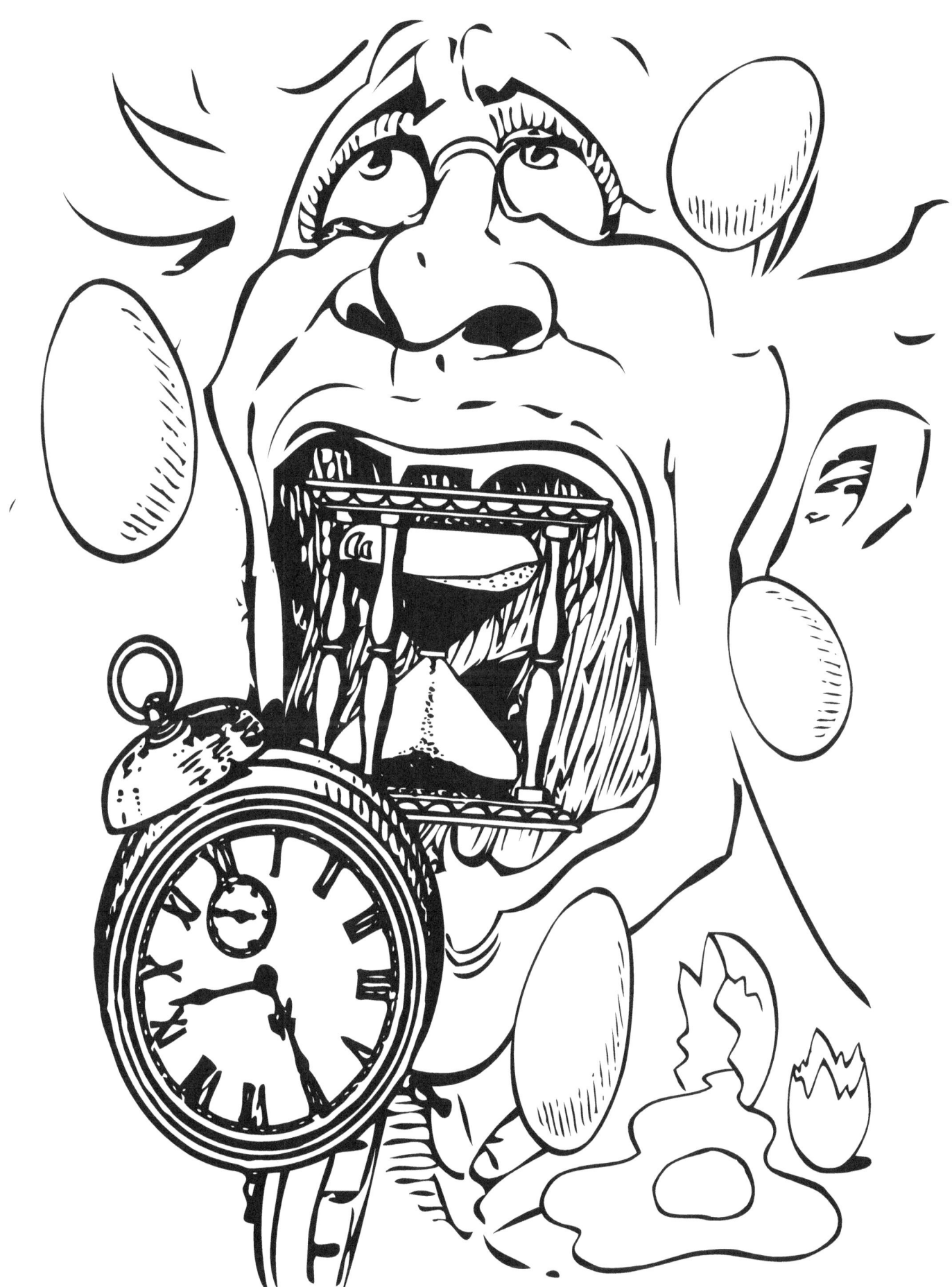

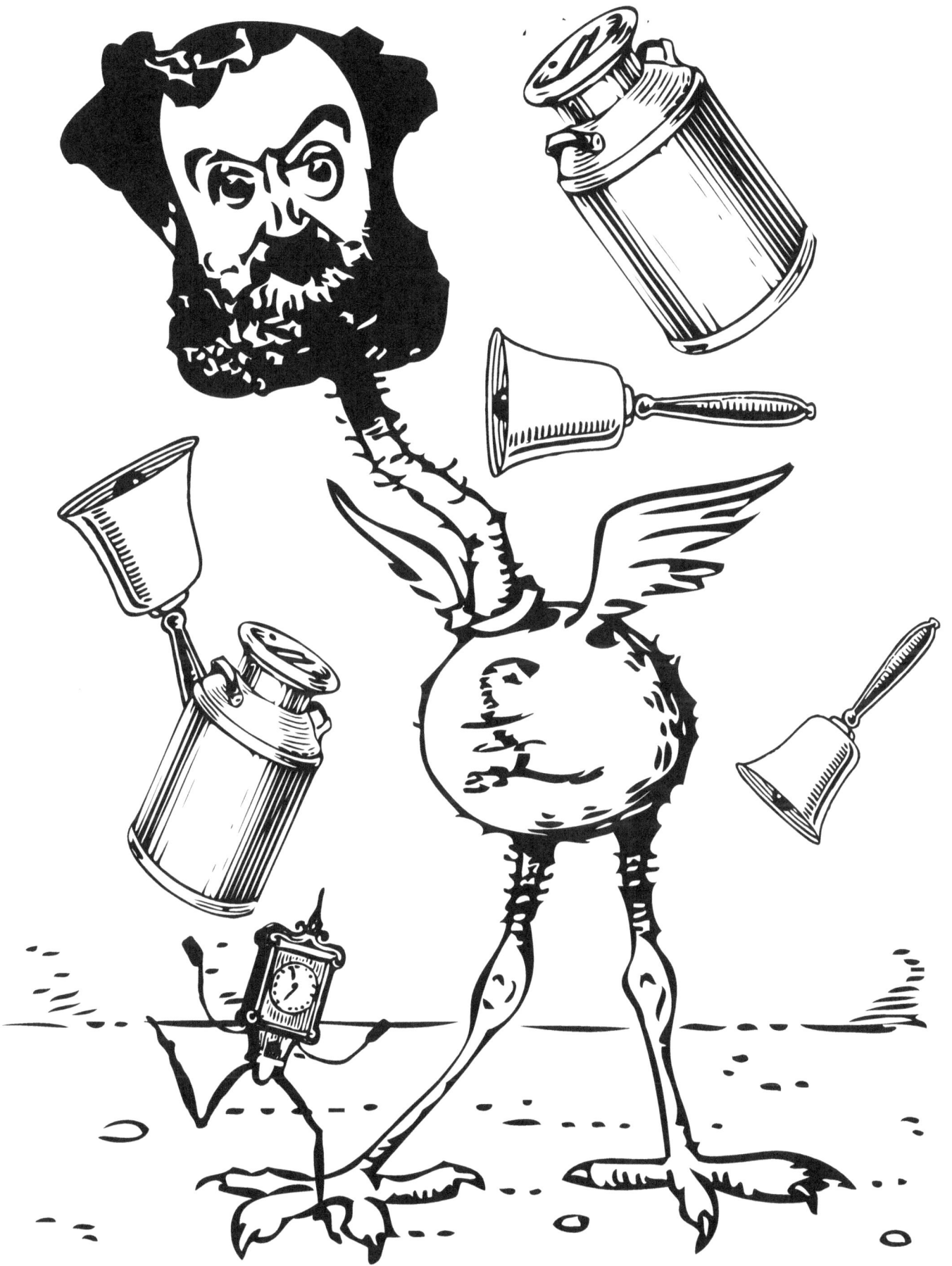

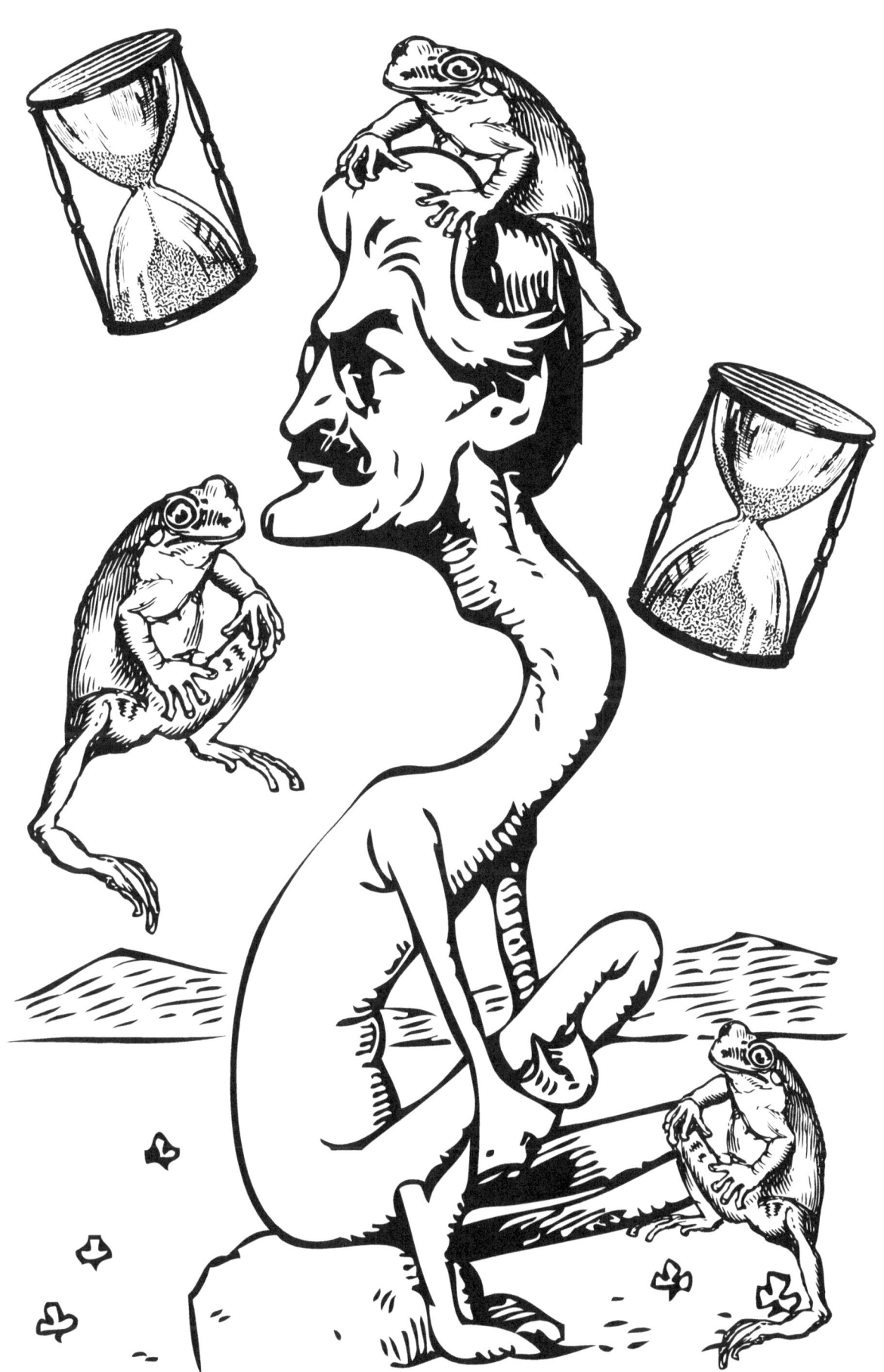

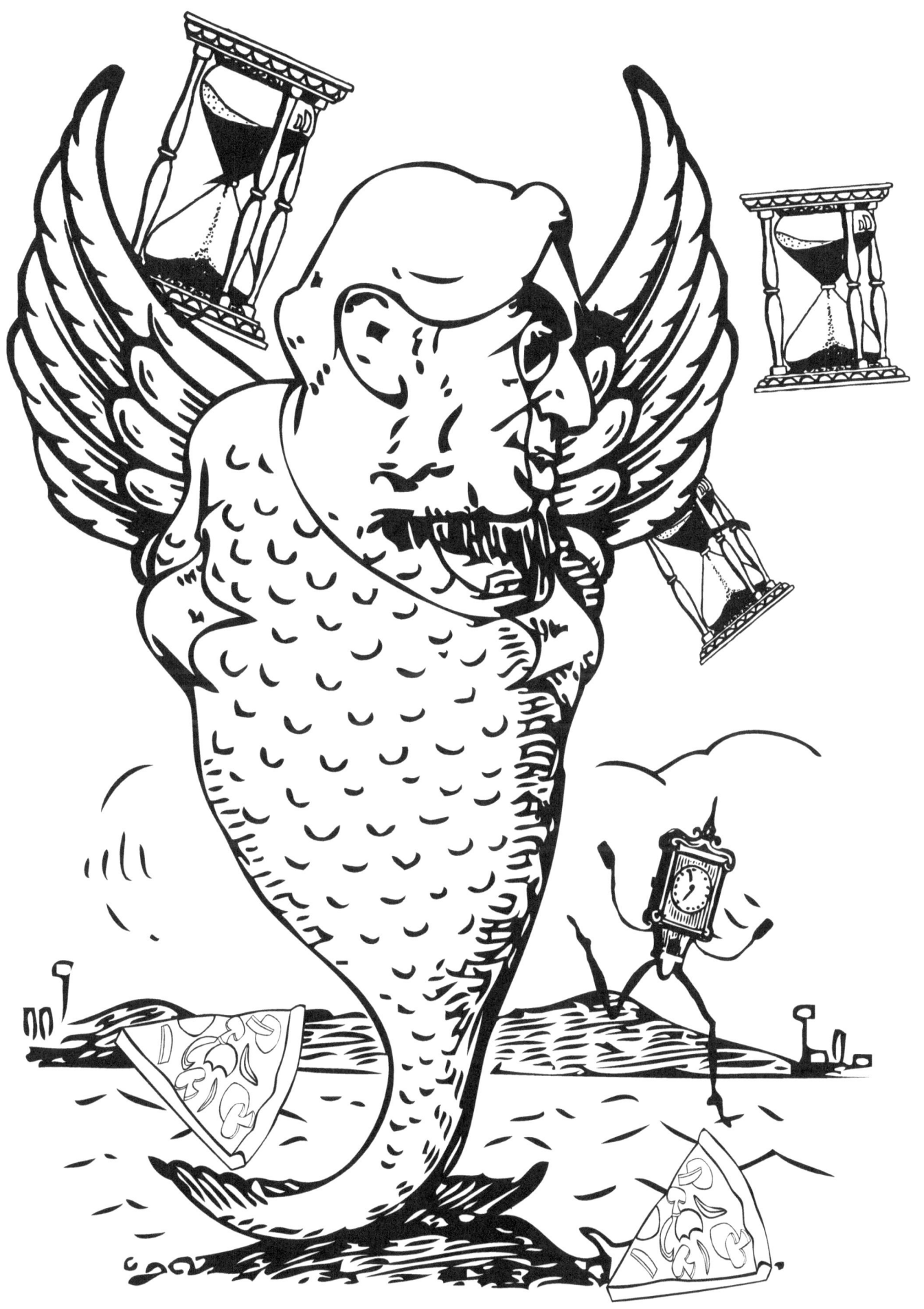

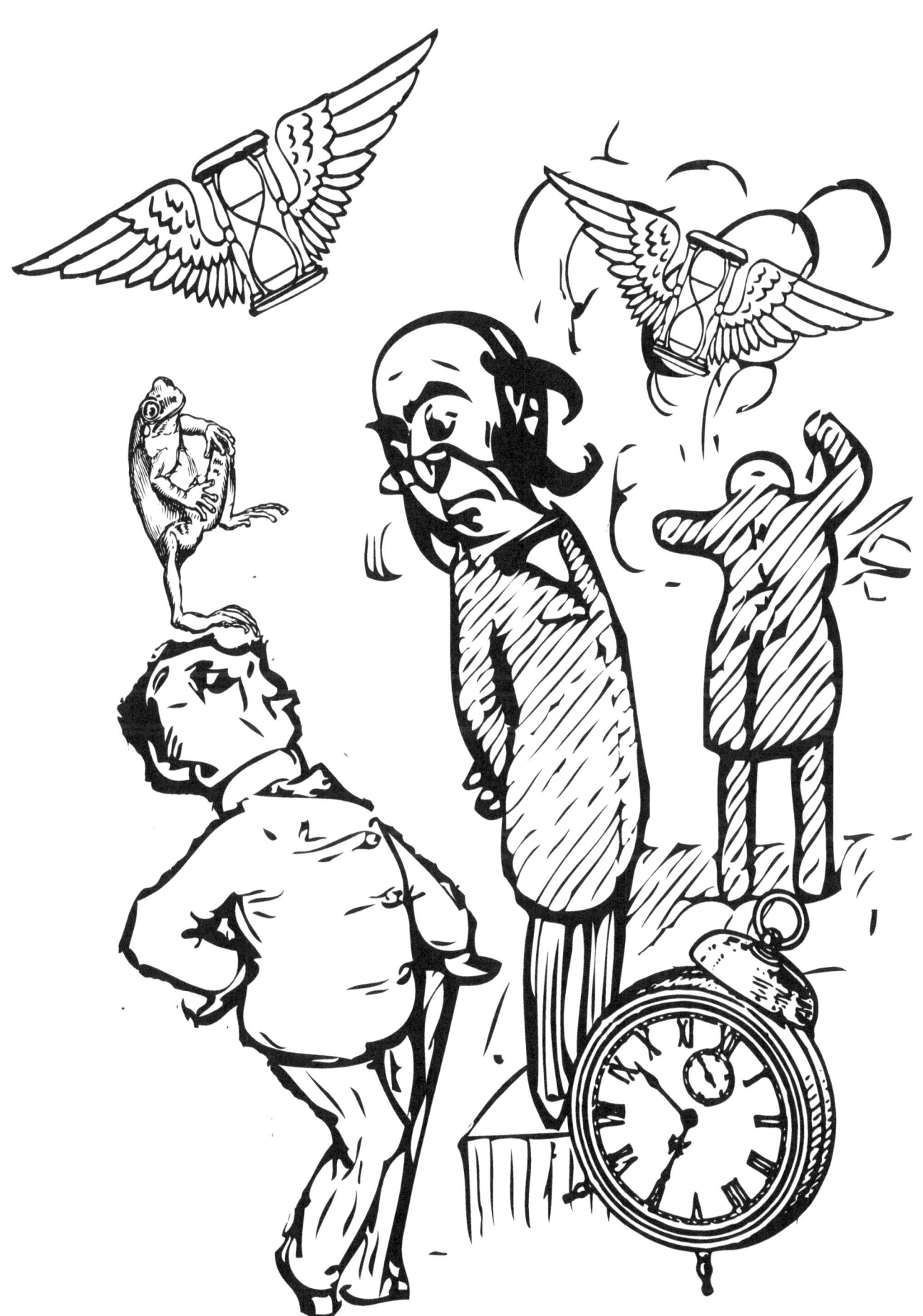

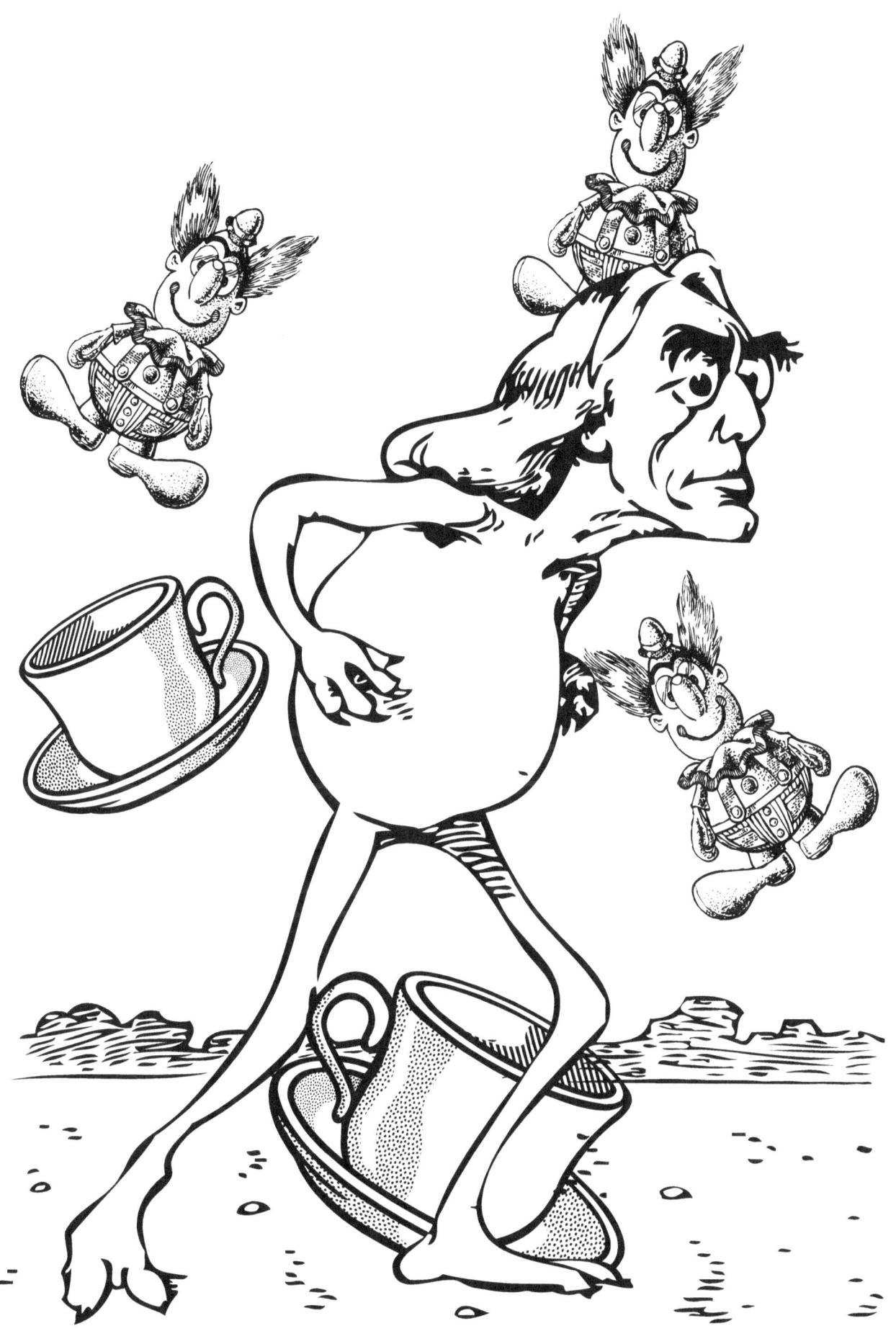

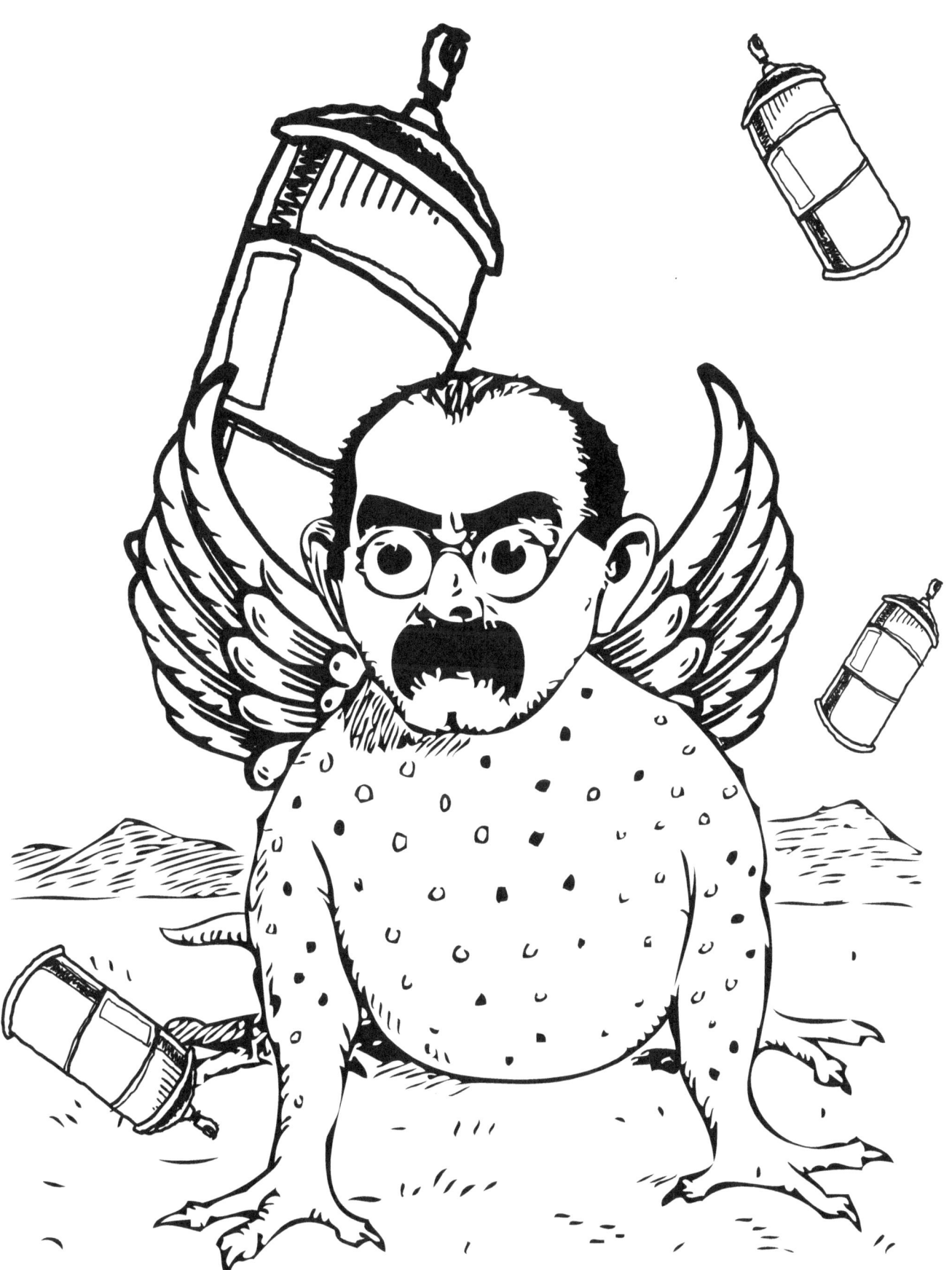

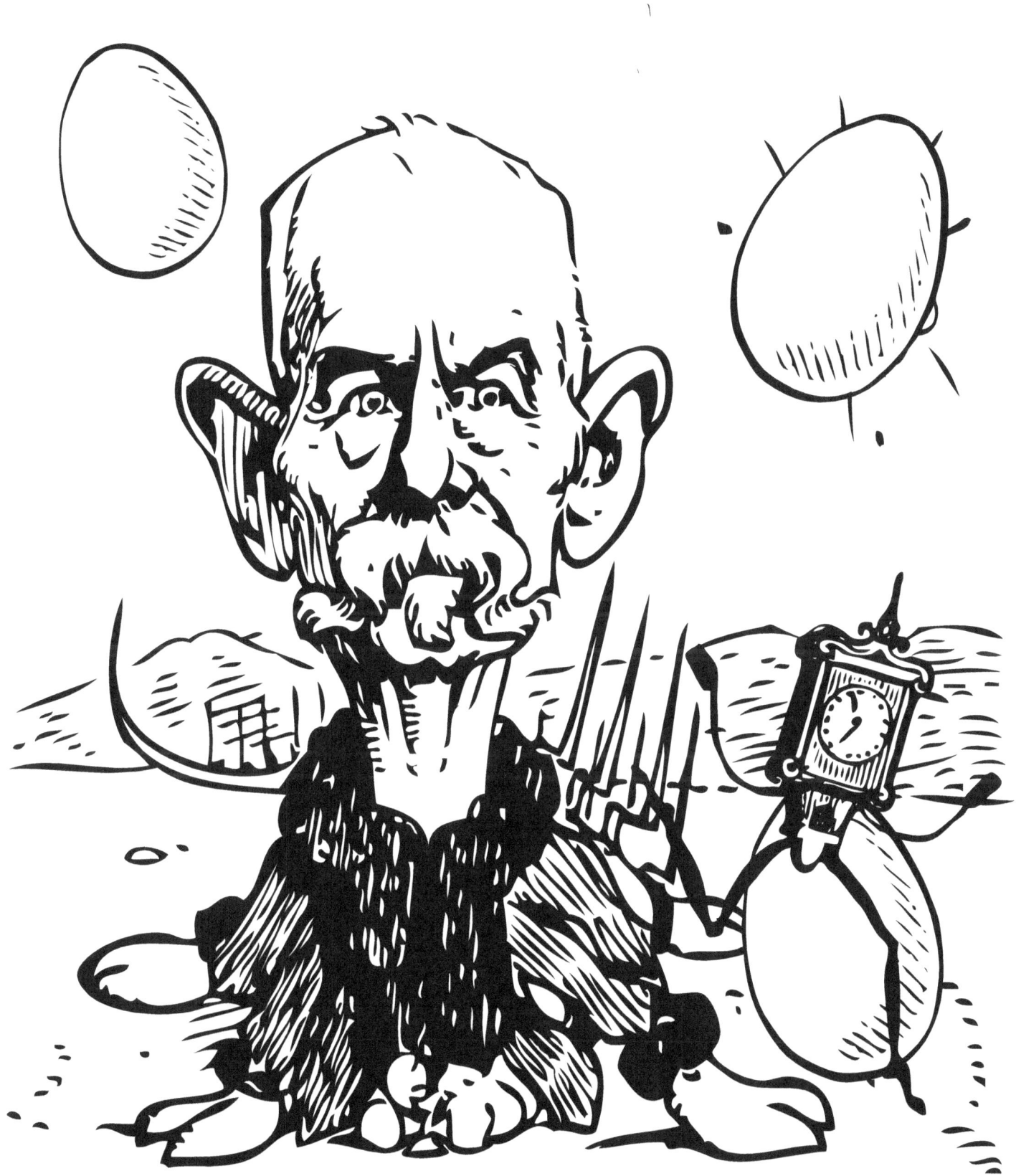

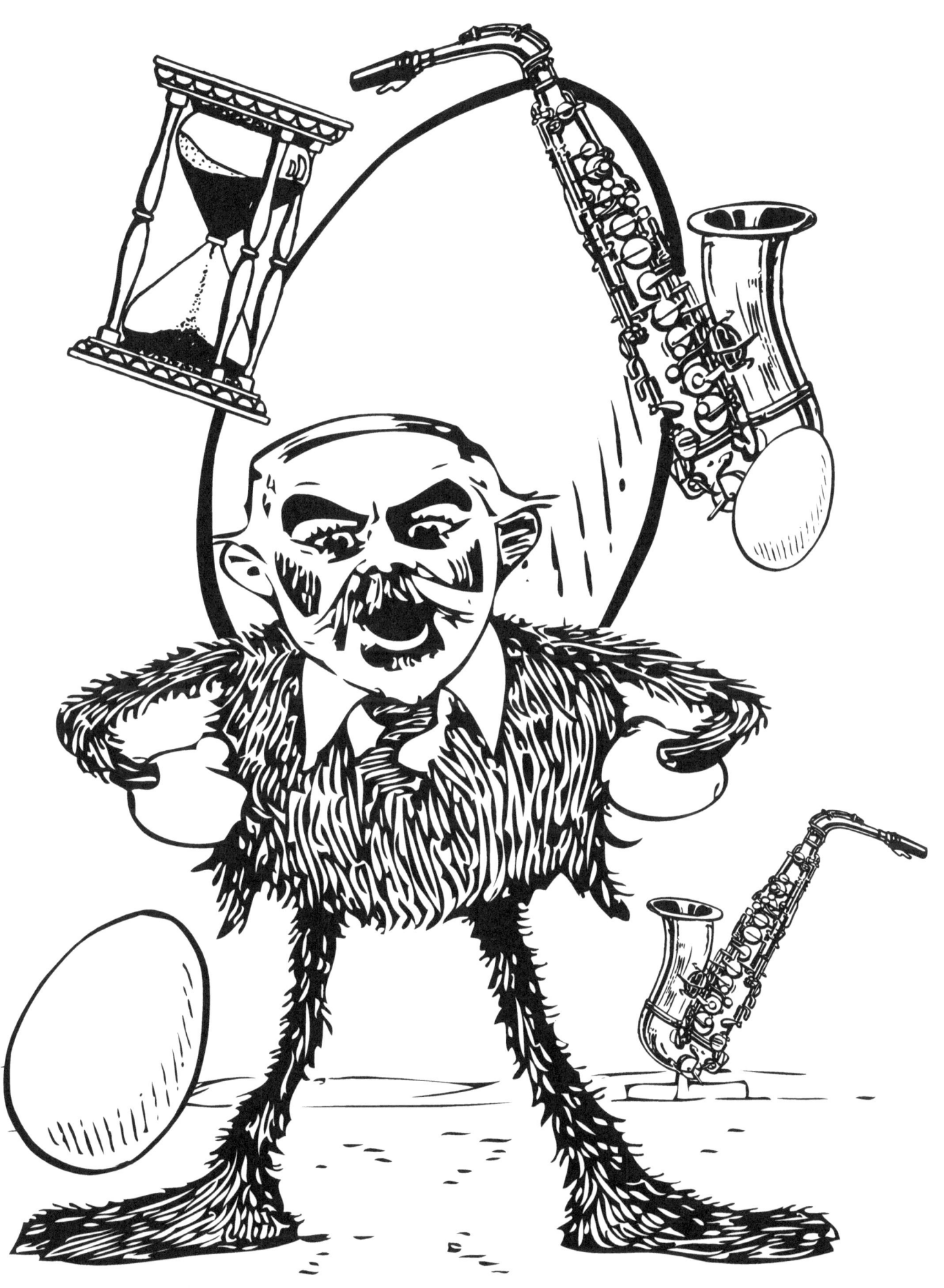

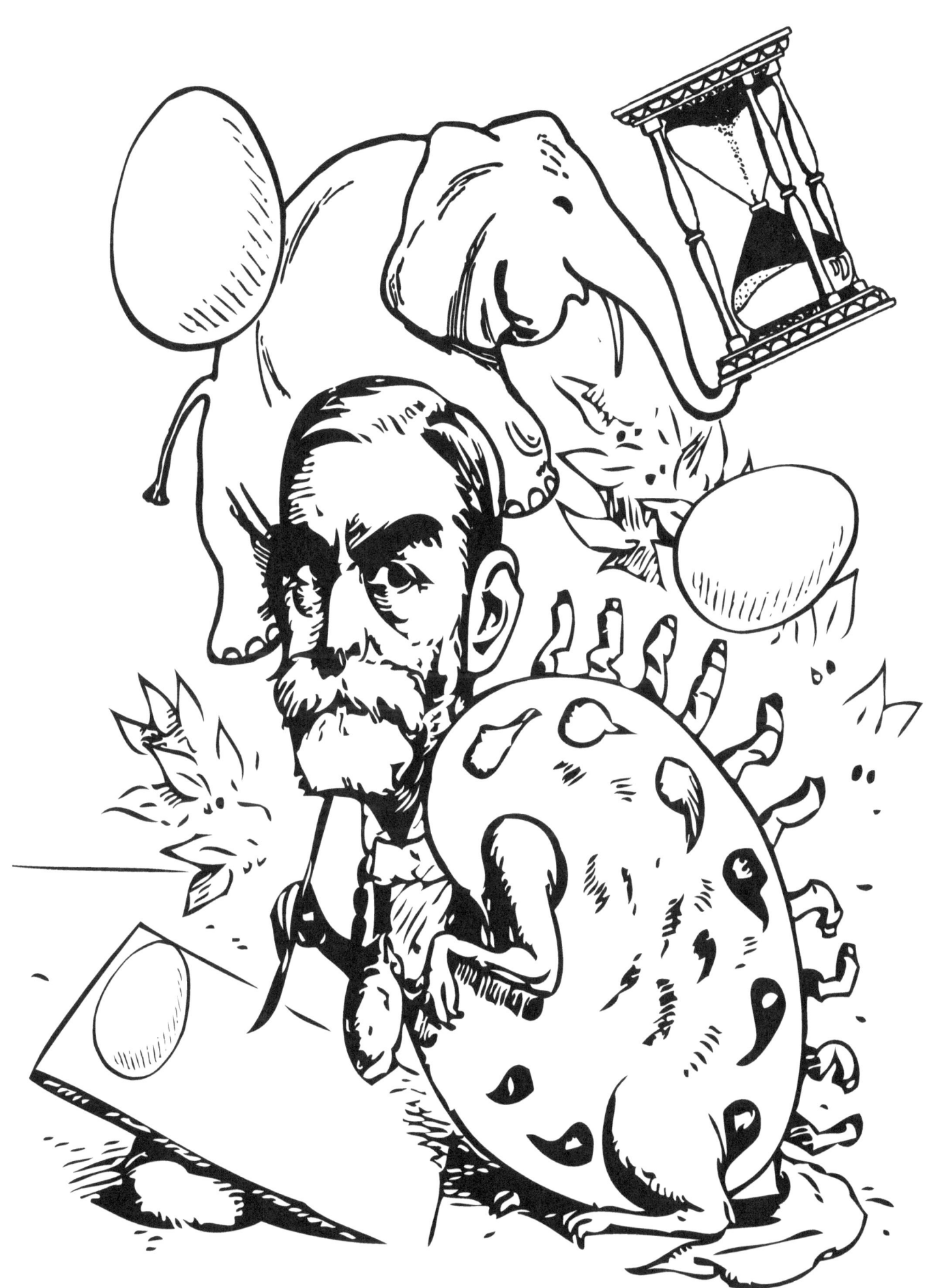

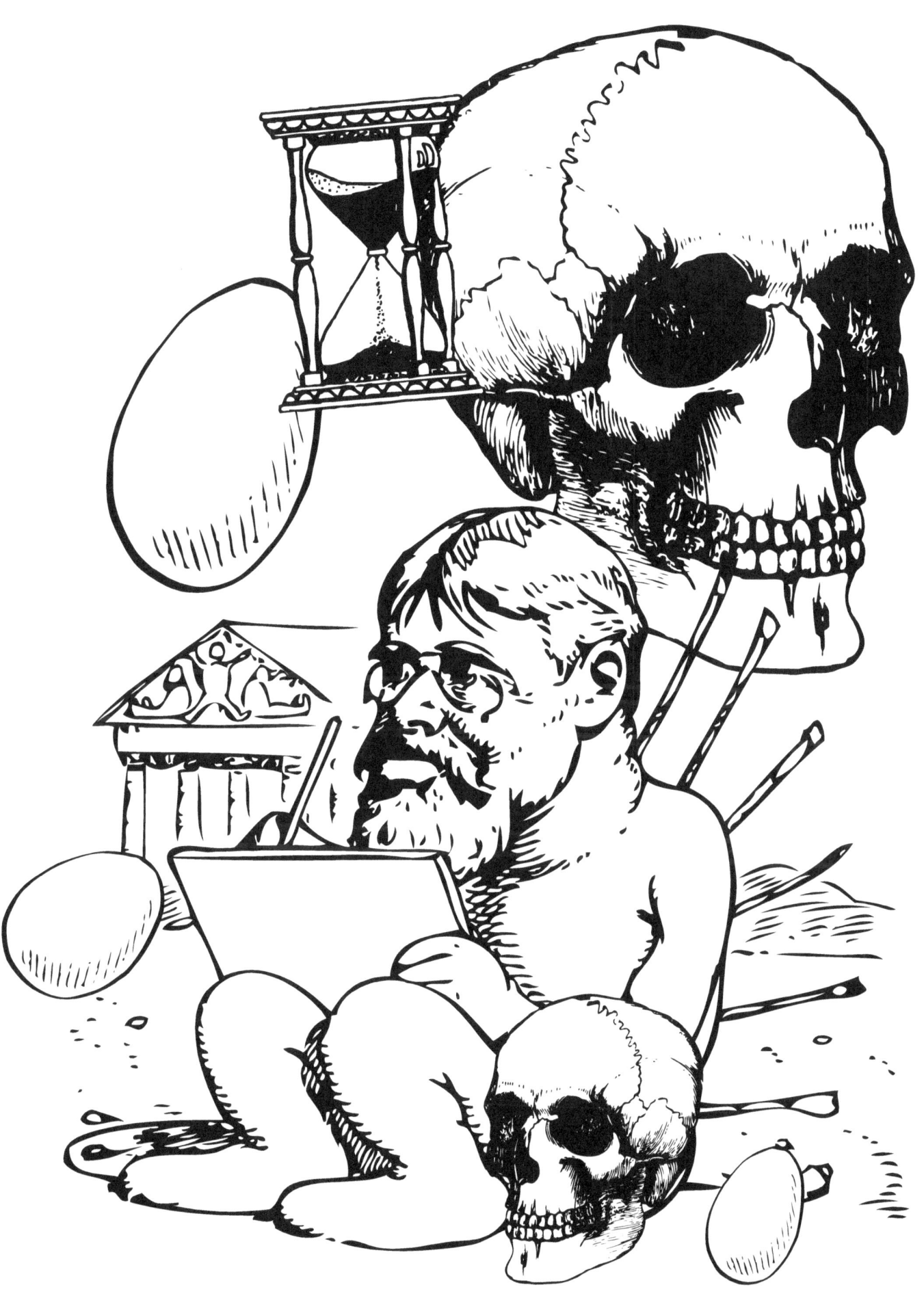

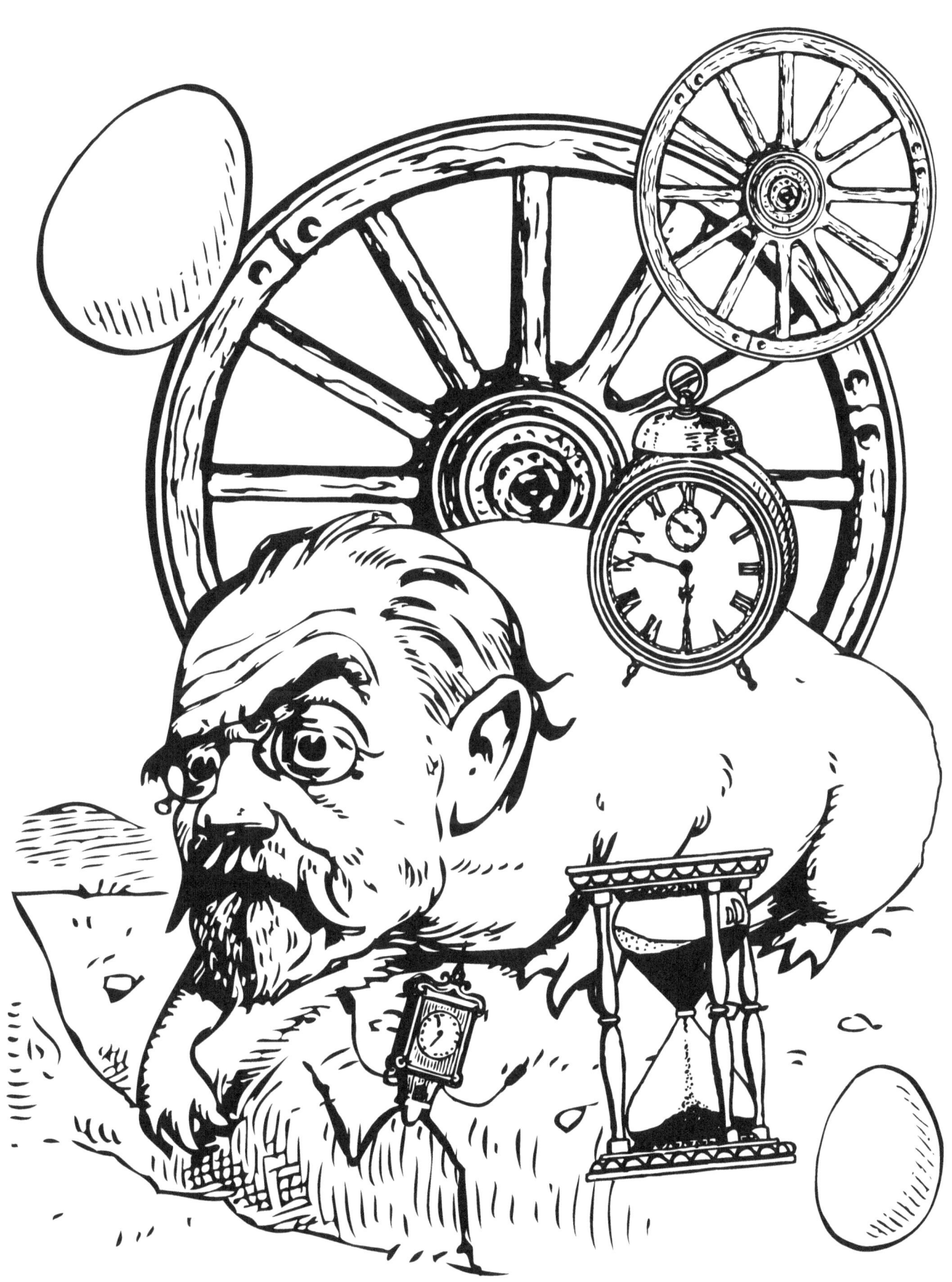

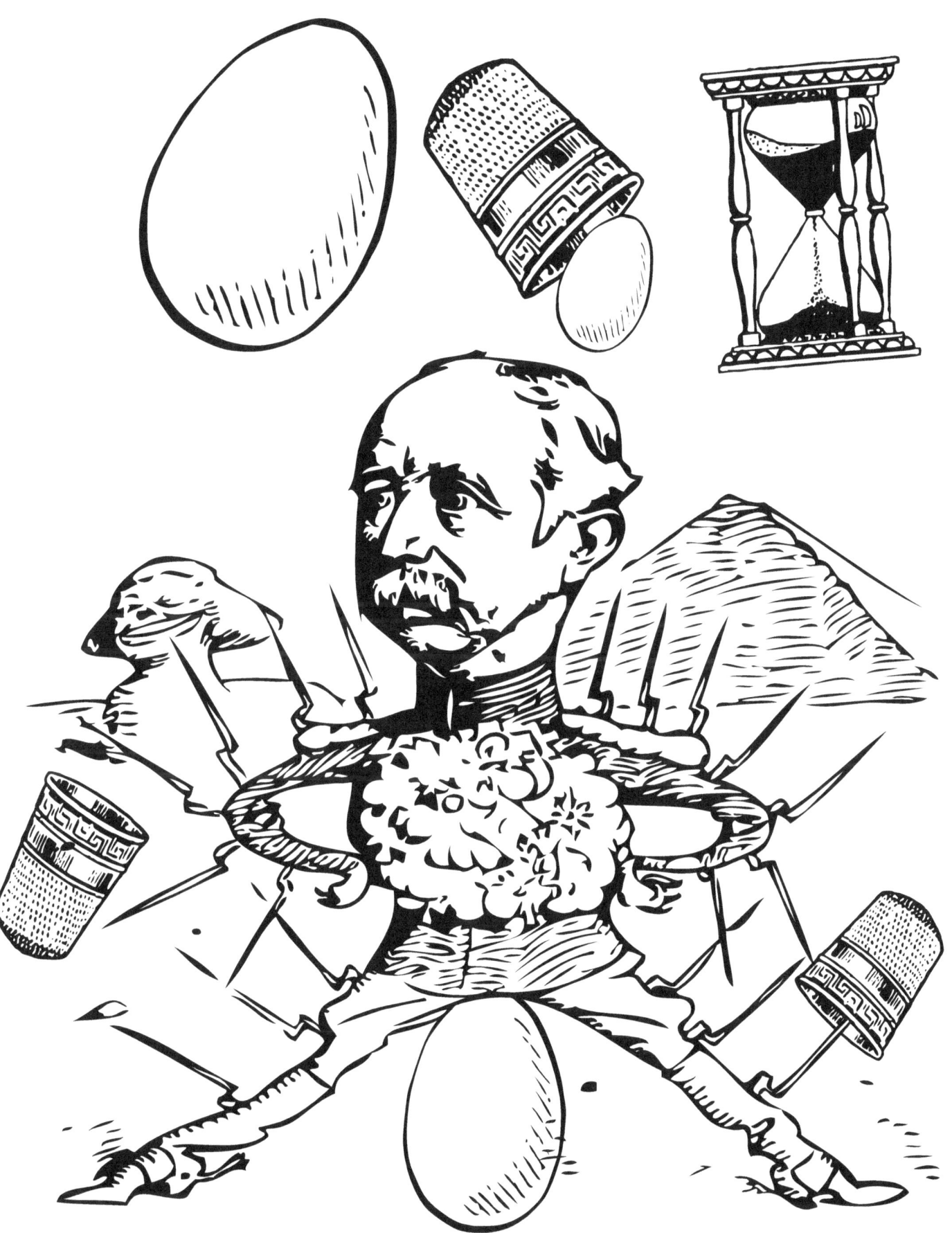

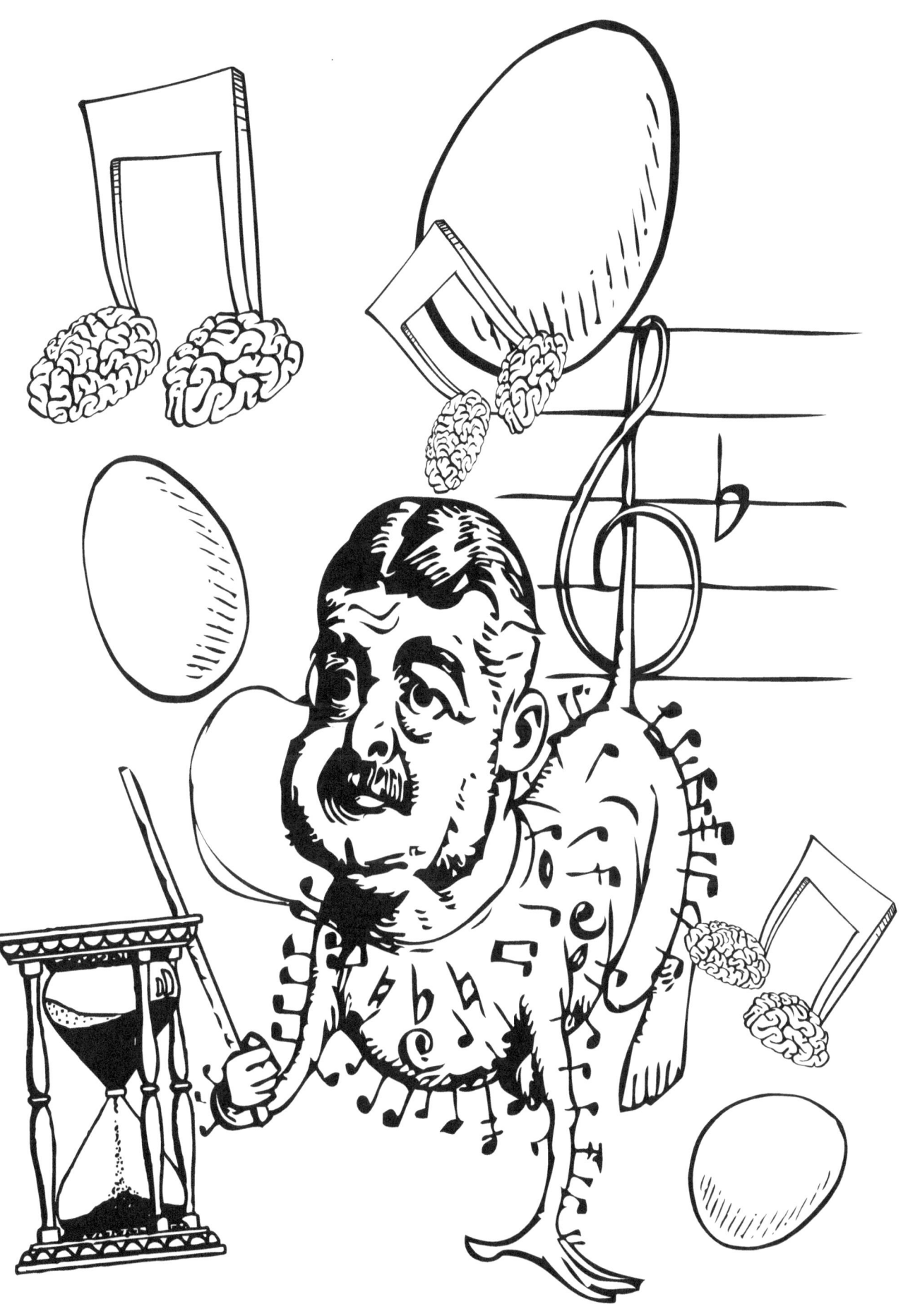

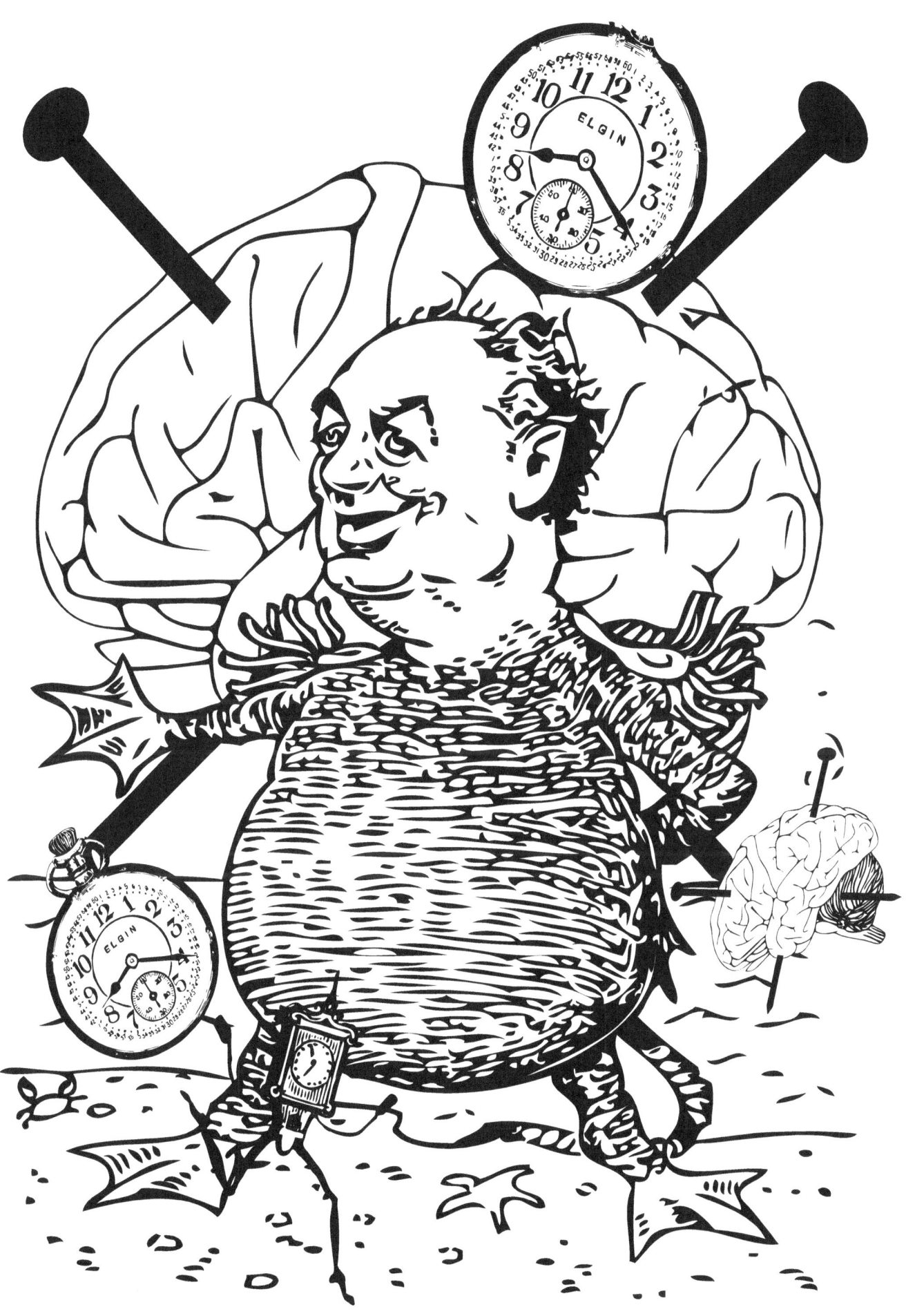

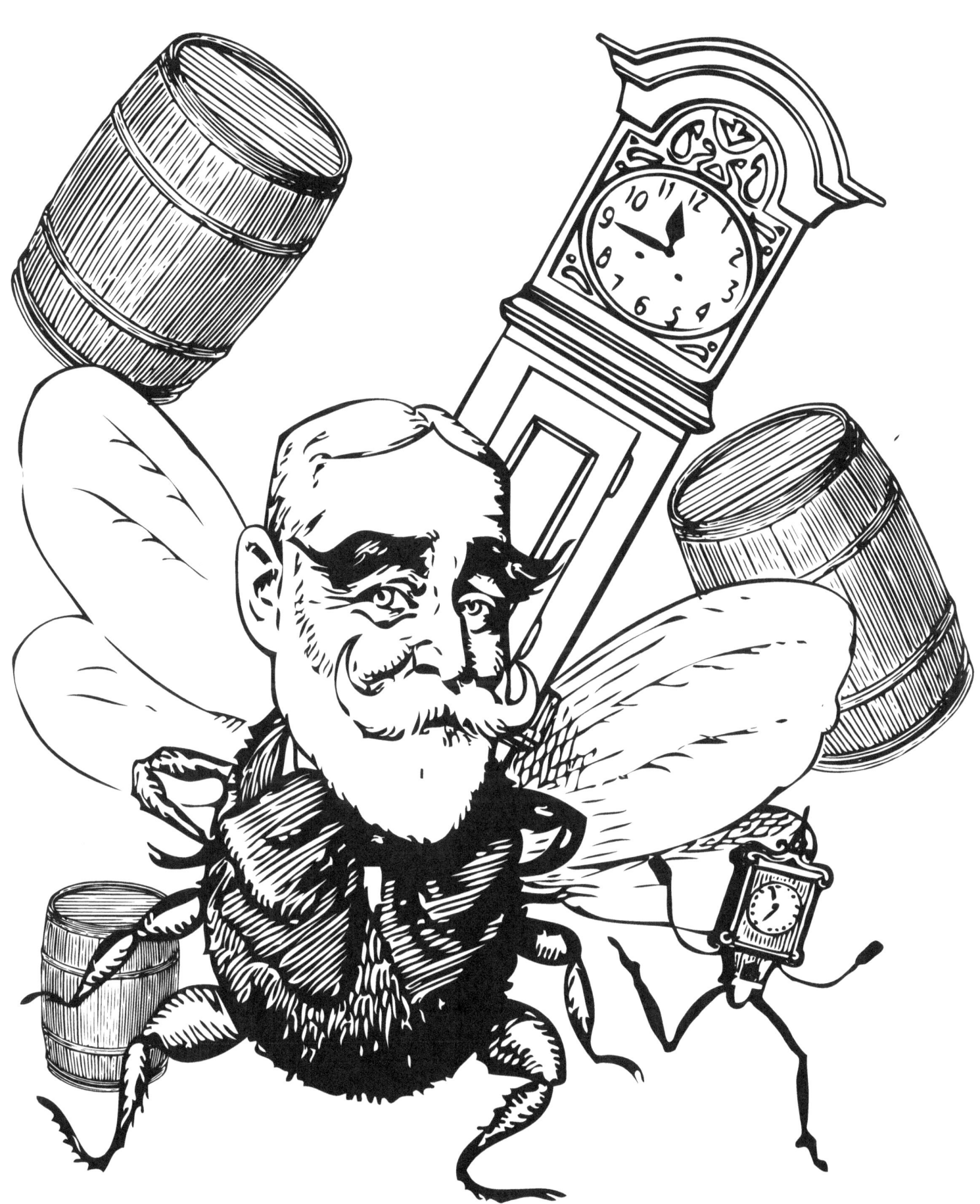

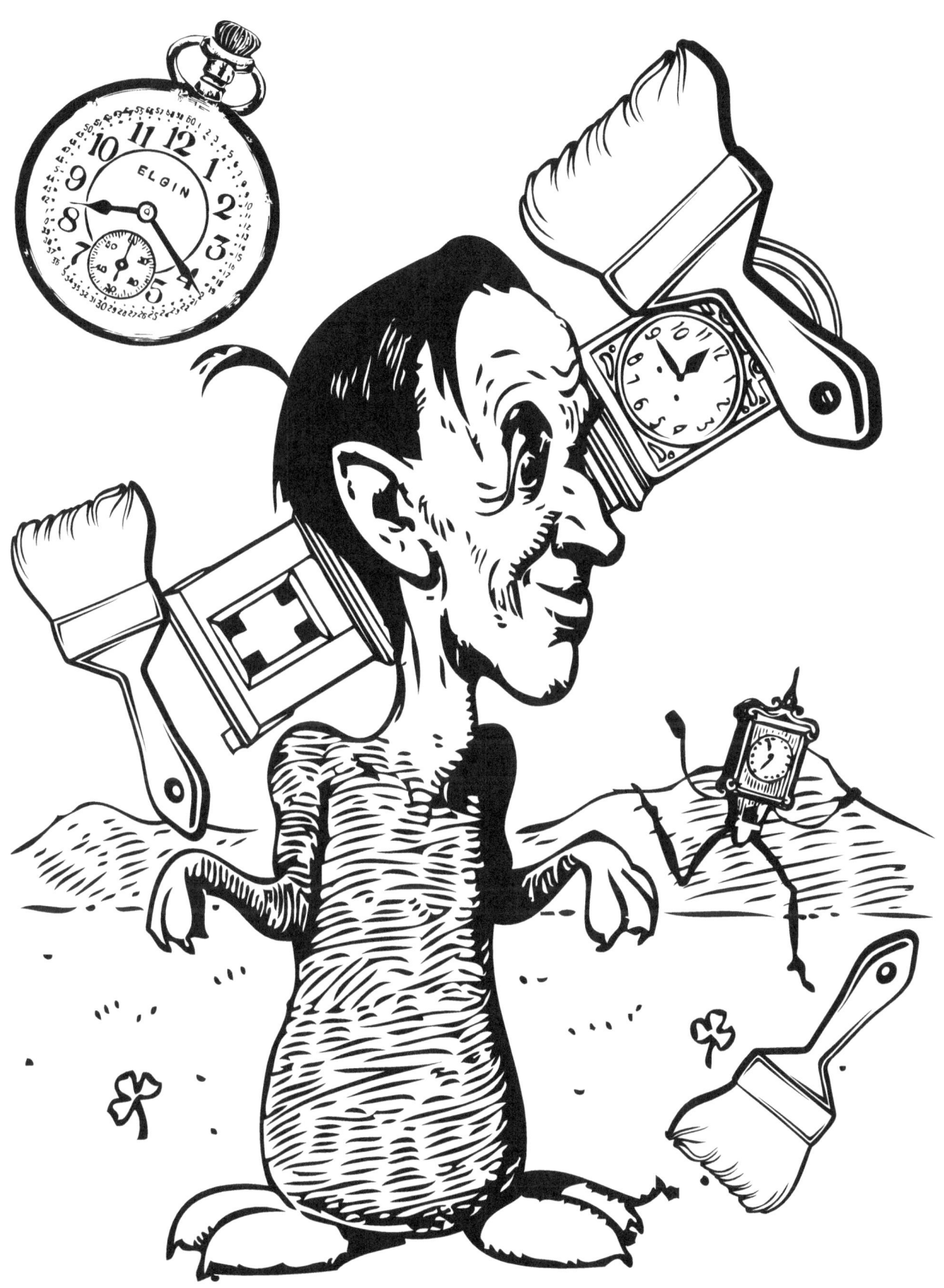

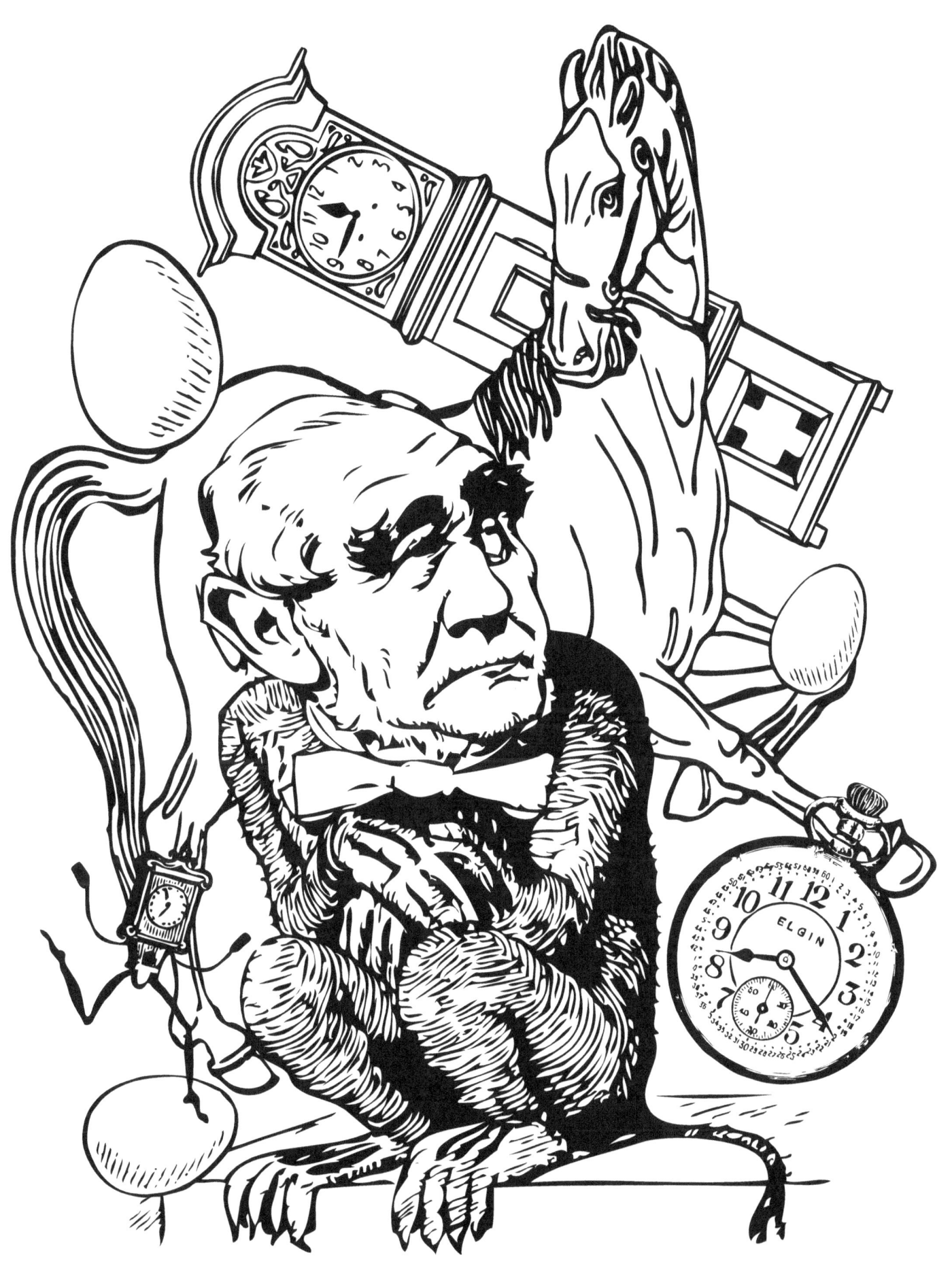

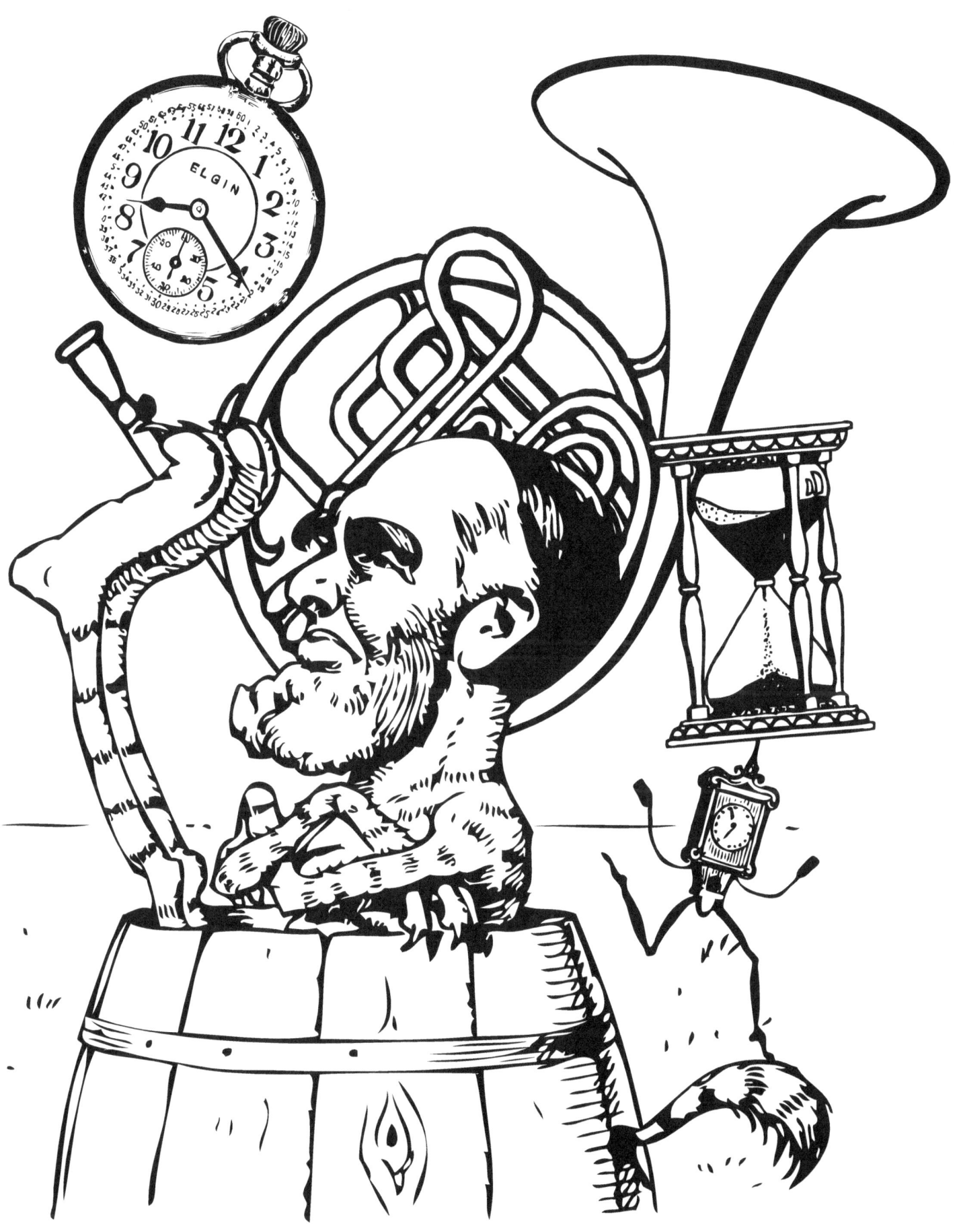

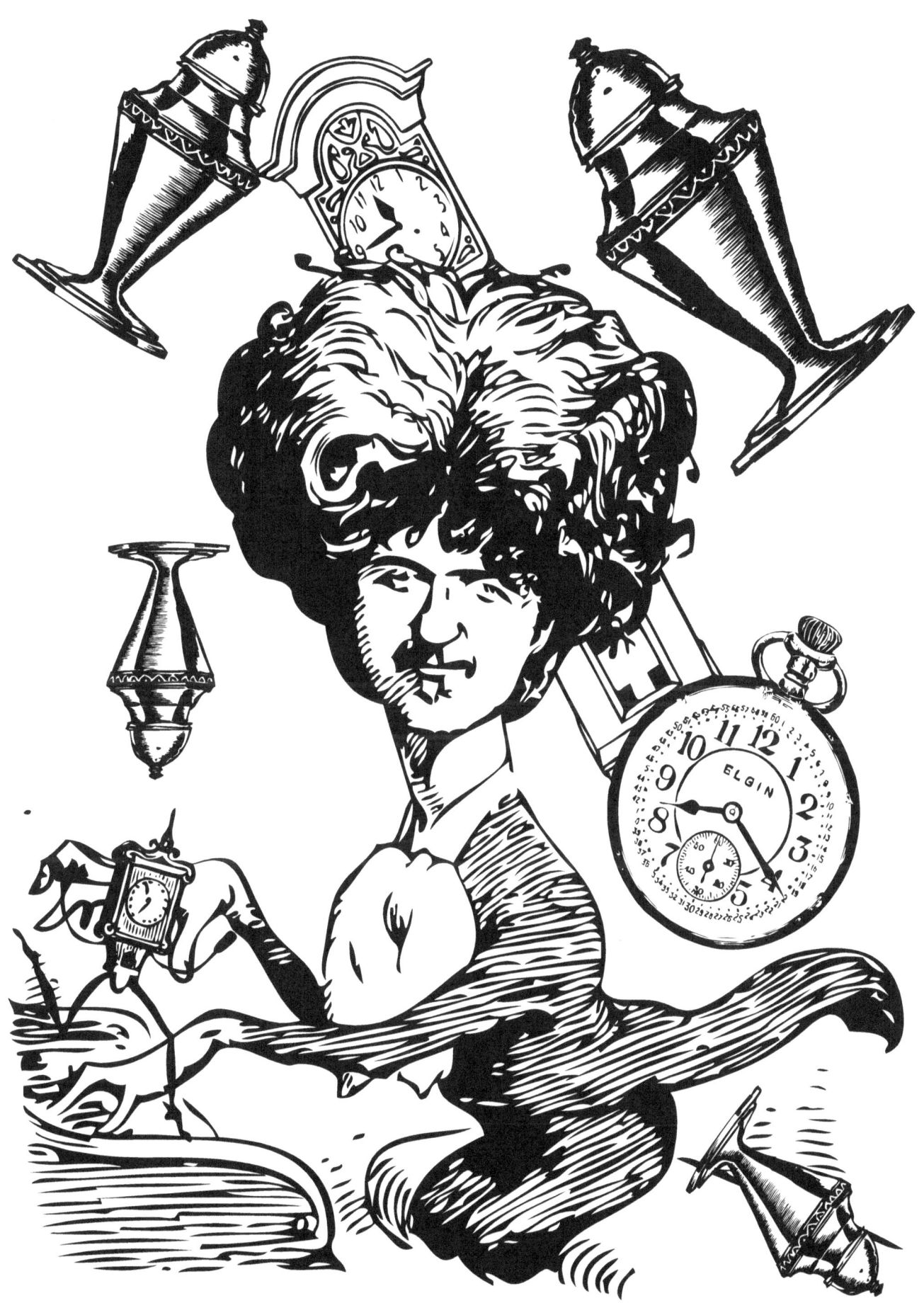

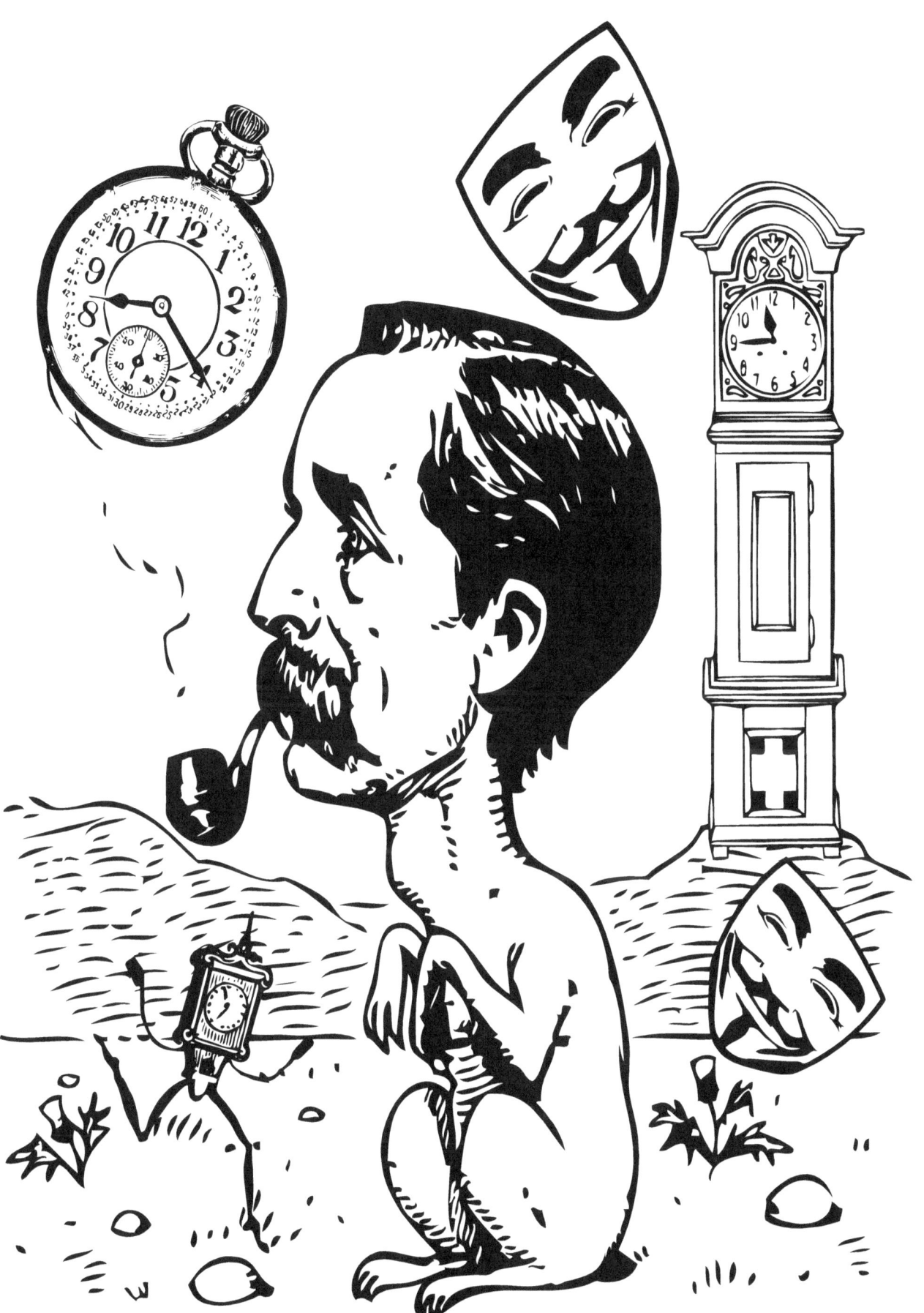

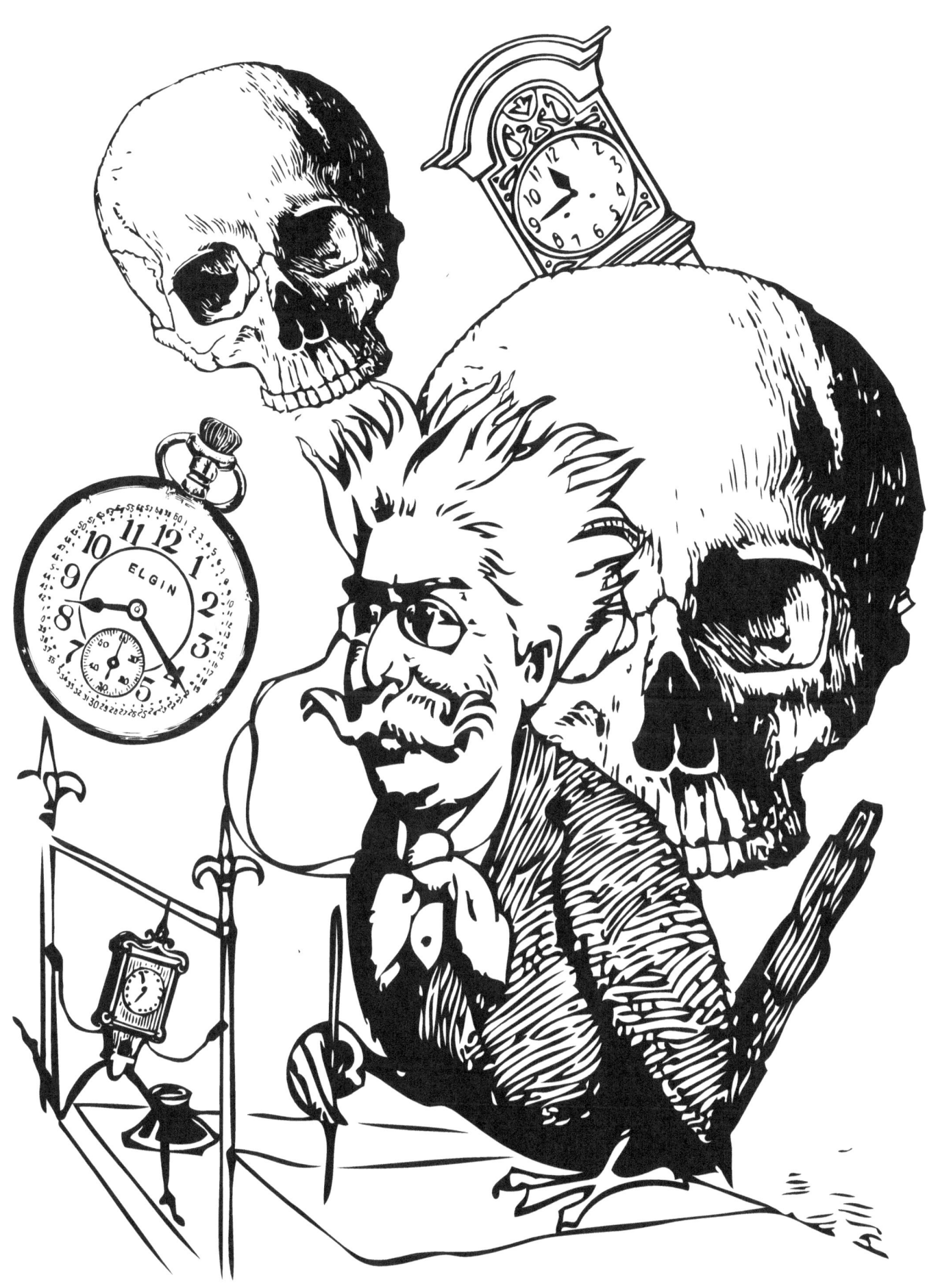

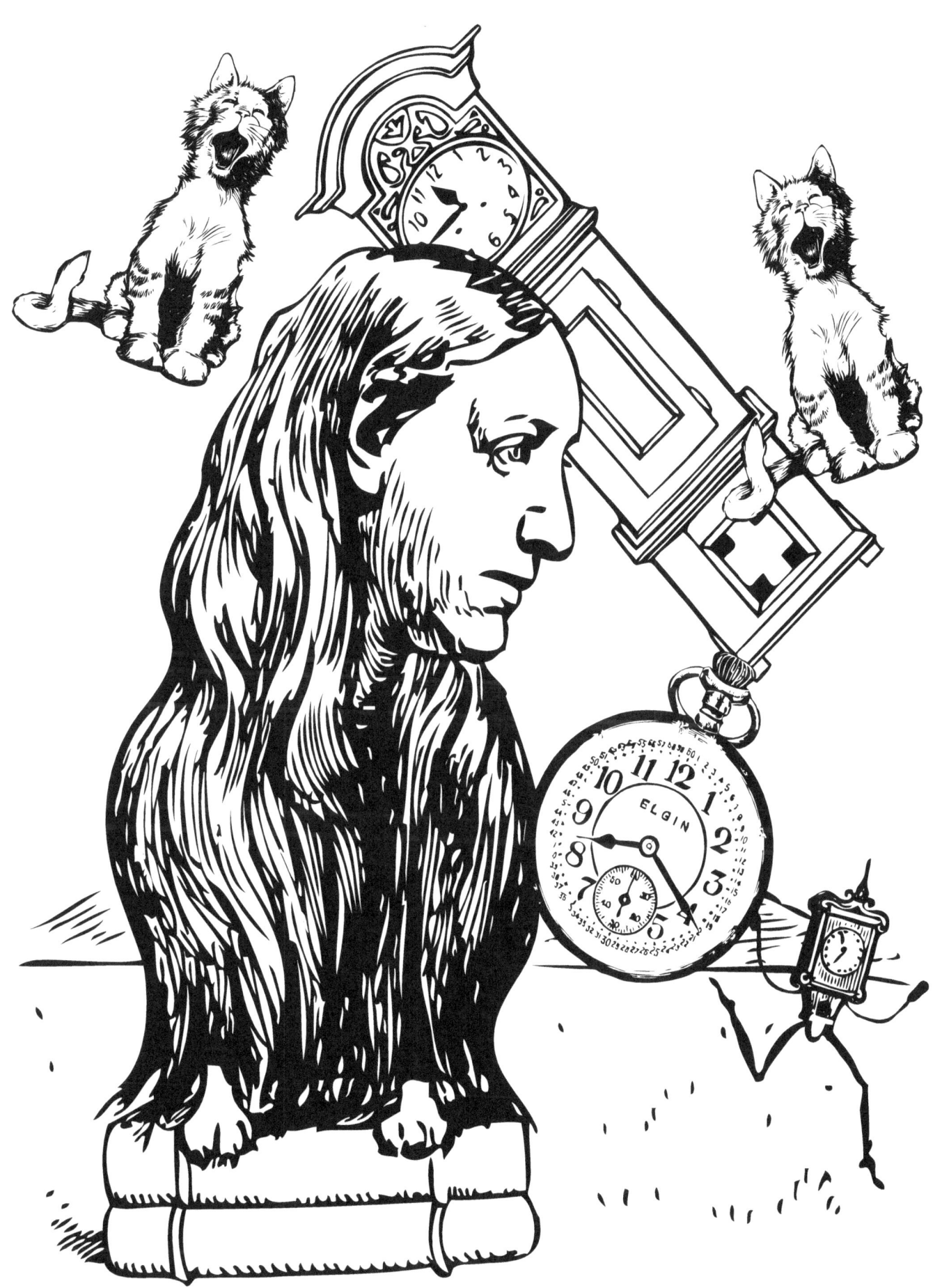

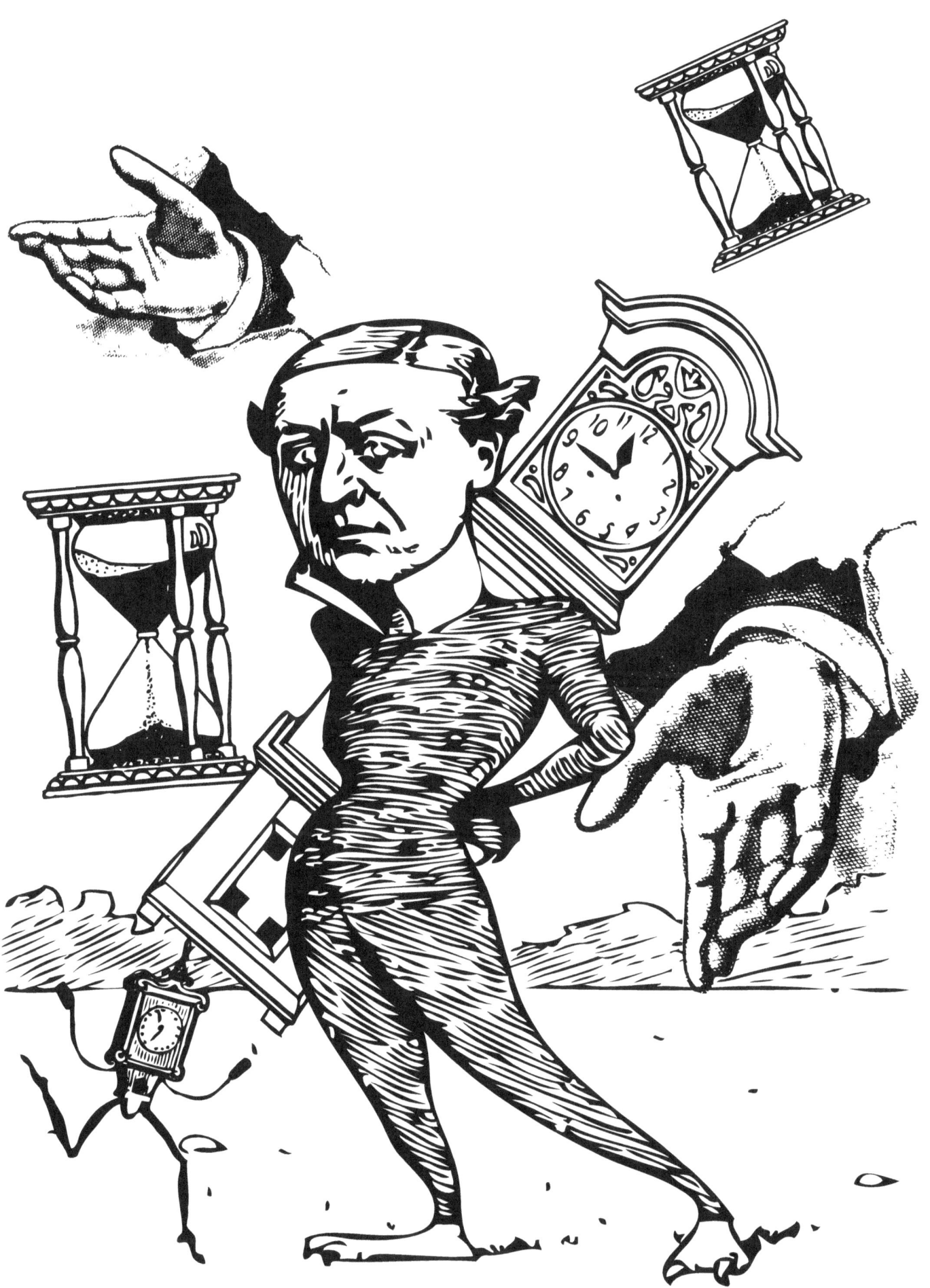

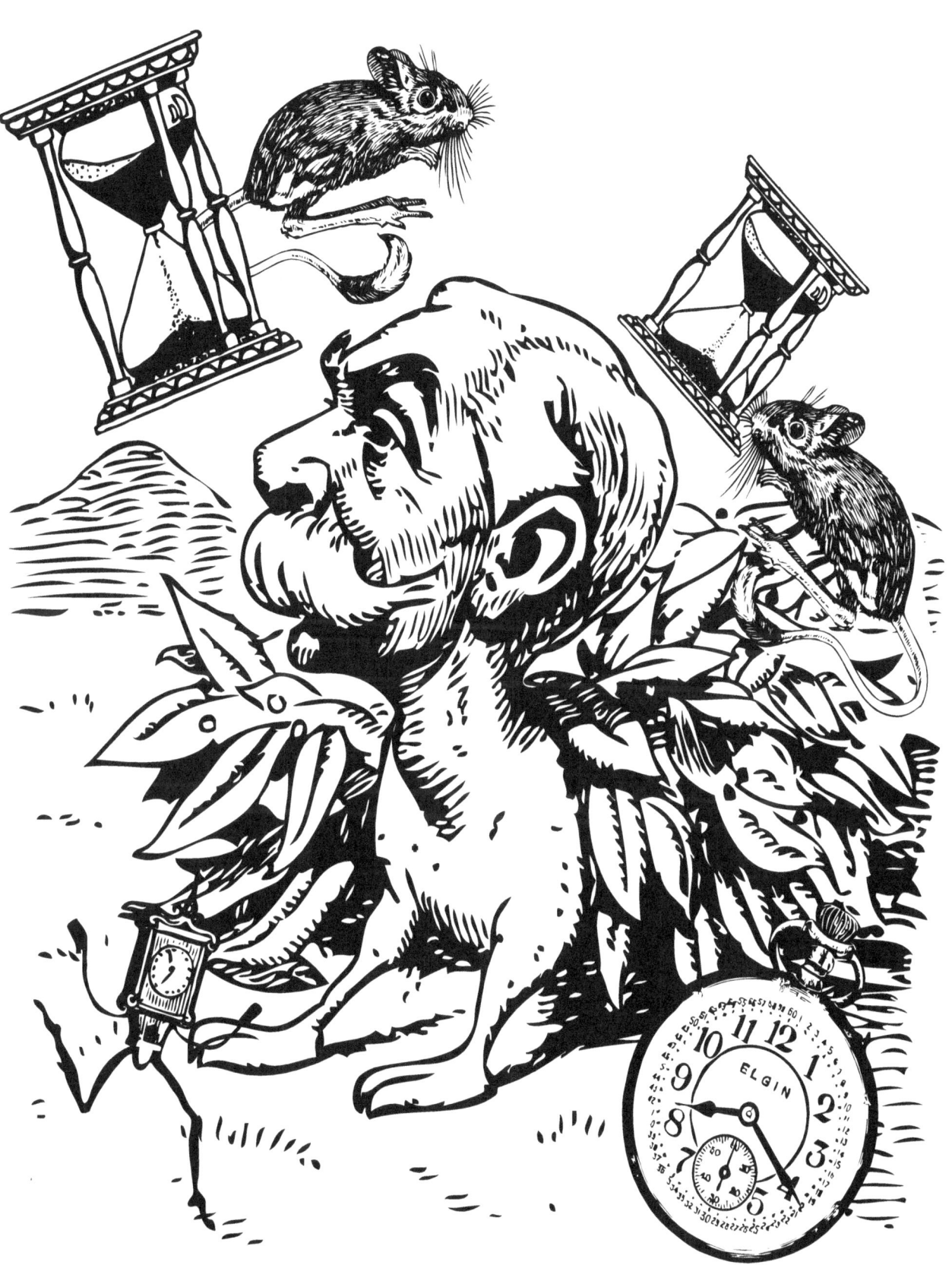

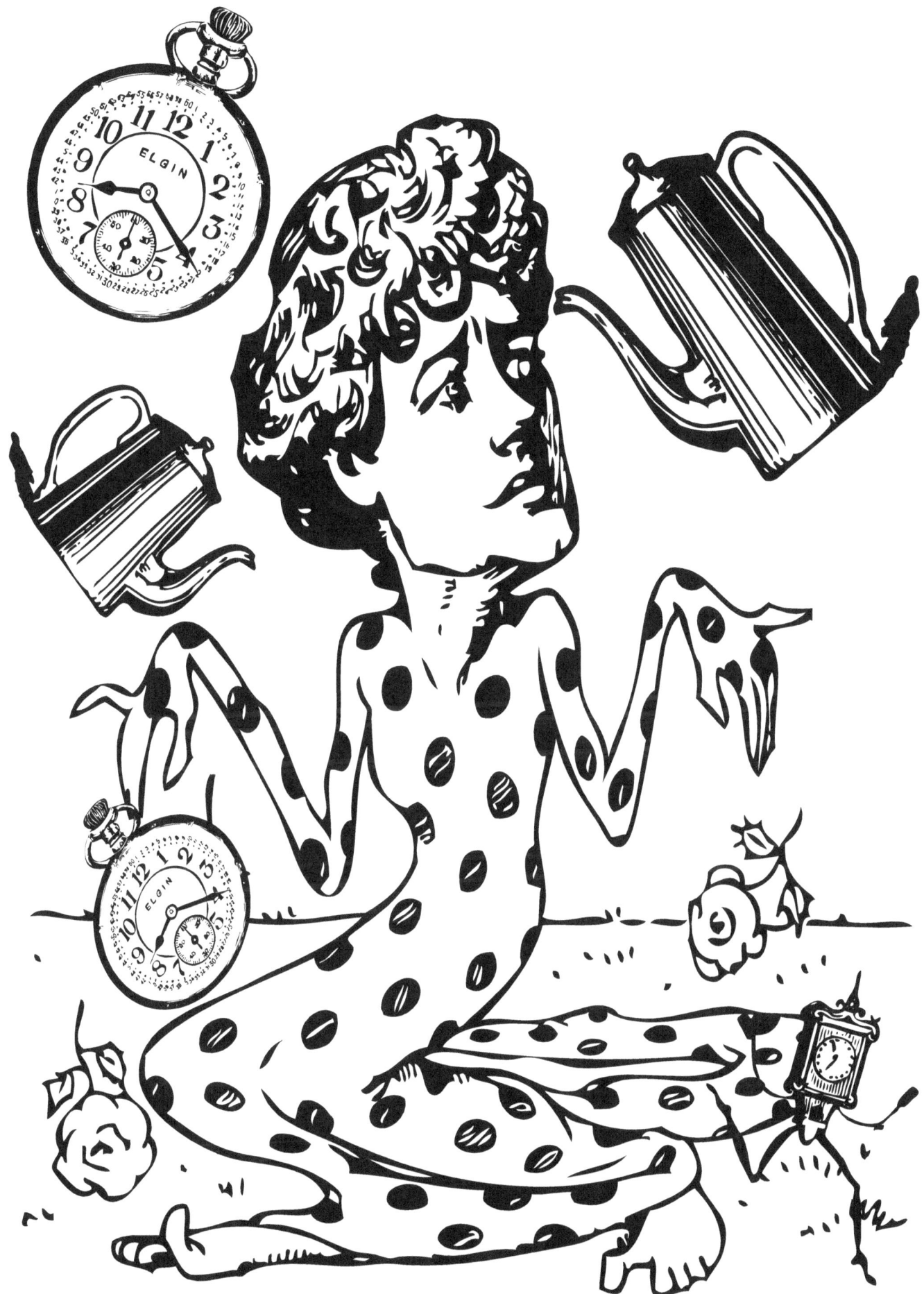

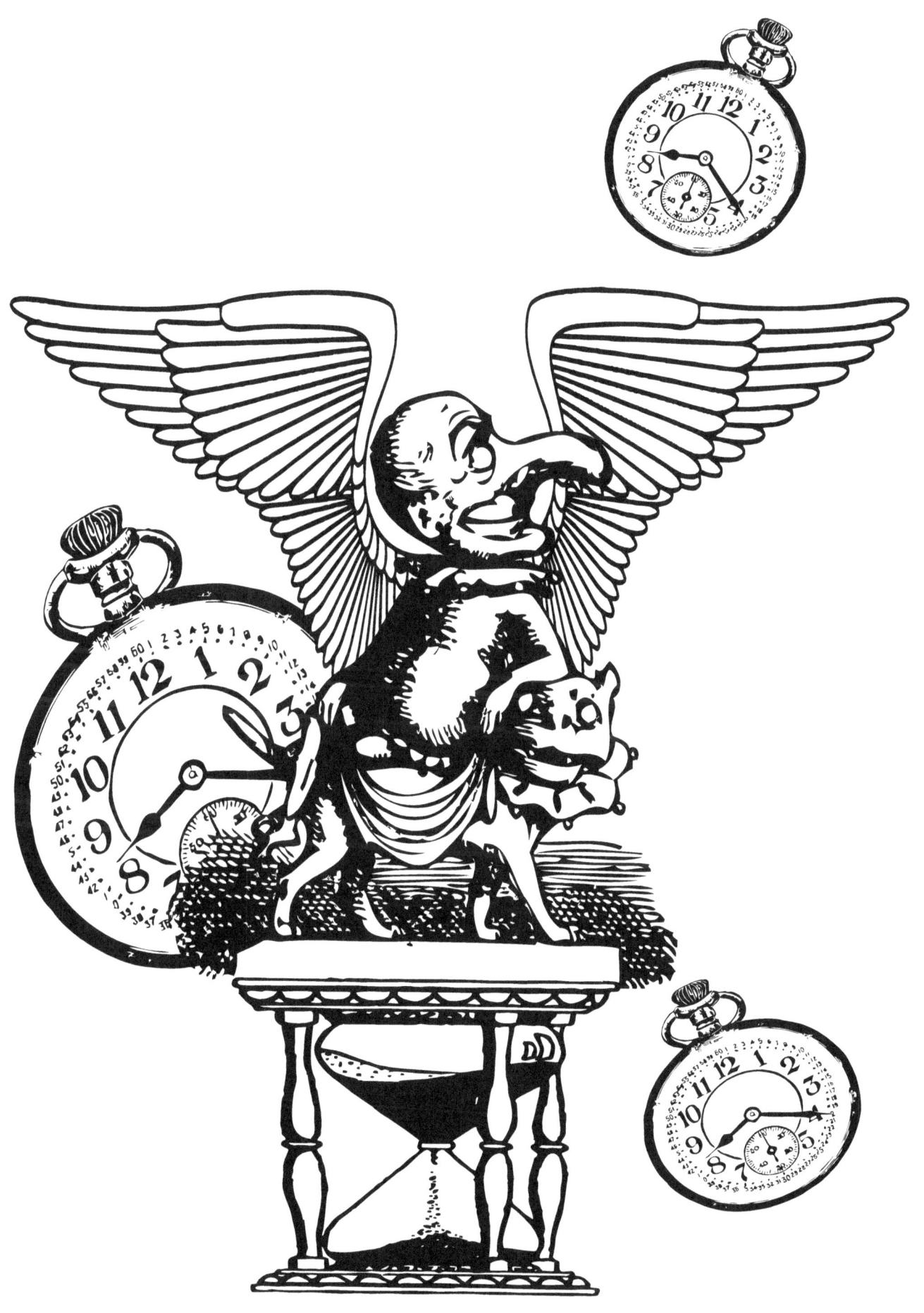